CH00651300

We would li
patience, ar
courage and
We would al:
her excellent

In addition, w
for their comments, knowledge, and encouragement
throughout the development of this product.

Linda F. Desmond, PMP
Project Management Training/Consulting

Fred DiLuzio, PhD, PMP
Director of Enterprise PMO
United Behavioral Health

David Gasso, MBA
SCE

Terri Gaydon, PMP
National Program Director, Sarbanes-Oxley
Kaiser Permanente

Linda L. Hallquist, PMP
Senior Instructor
American Family Insurance Group

Karen McCombs
Director, Curriculum Development
The Institute of Internal Auditors

Charles "Skip" Pettit, MEd, CRC
President
International Training Consortium, Inc.

How to Use This Book

This book uses visual cues, examples, design features, and clear, friendly language to help align all of the project professionals in your organization to support organizational project performance. Whether you use this book as a reference or as a supplement to training, we trust that you will see an improvement in your organization's effectiveness in managing and controlling projects.

To Find a Topic

Use the table of contents at the front of the book, or the chart at the beginning of every chapter (shown below).

When you need to: ➡ Check the section on:

To Find the Start of Each Chapter

Look for the blue box at the bottom of the page.

To See at a Glance Which Activities May Be of Interest to You

Look for the name badge icons (shown below) in each section to see who would most benefit from the accompanying information. (Although the activity in the section may be of interest to any individual involved in a project, regardless of his or her title or project role, the icons are intended to show that the particular activity in the section will be of primary interest to the specific project professionals listed. An overview at the end of the Introduction also shows which chapters will be of primary and secondary interest to particular audiences.)

The
Advanced Project Management
MEMORY JOGGER™

A Pocket Guide for
Experienced Project Professionals

Karen Tate, PMP
and
Cynthia Stackpole, PMP

GOAL/QPC

The Advanced Project Management Memory Jogger™

Development Team

Karen Tate, *Author*
Cynthia Stackpole, *Author*
Daniel Picard, *Project Leader, Technical Editor*
Michele Kierstead, *Cover & Book Design*

GOAL/QPC

12B Manor Parkway, Salem, NH 03079-2862

Toll free: 800-643-4316 **or** 603-893-1944
Fax: 603-870-9122
E-mail: service@goalqpc.com
Web site: www.goalqpc.com

Printed in the United States of America

First Edition
10 9 8 7 6 5 4 3 2 1

ISBN 10: 1-57681-086-0
ISBN 13: 978-1-57681-086-6

To Find Tips & Pitfalls

 Look for the sections on gray backgrounds, with the icon shown.

To Find Examples that are Illustrated Through the Book

Look for graphics that have a graph paper fill in them.

To Find Additional Information on Included Topics

Look for the sections on blue backgrounds. These sections provide important information to better explain the concepts included in the chapter and assist in helping you to better understand the ideas, tools, and techniques you will use as you further your organization's project management performance.

Contents

Introduction

Welcome to *The Advanced Project Management Memory Jogger™*. Our goal is to help you achieve more successful projects. To that end, we describe the "what" and "how"—as well as the "why"—of best-practice project management techniques.

This book is for people who have been involved with projects for some time:

- Experienced project managers

- Project sponsors

- Executives who manage the project portfolio by selecting, prioritizing, and steering projects

- Senior managers with accountability for projects or project management

- Project team members and subproject team leaders

At this point in your career you know a lot about:

- Defining scope

- Creating schedules

- Developing budget estimates

- Developing project management plans

- Monitoring progress

- Managing change

- Closing a project

The information in this book is consistent with that in GOAL/QPC's original *Project Management Memory Jogger™* (PMMJ). This book adds to and builds on topics in the PMMJ (such as defining scope and creating schedules) and introduces new topics such as establishing a project office, controlling projects, improving team communication, conducting negotiations, and enhancing leadership skills.

This book is for experienced project professionals. For beginning project managers and as a refresher for the experienced, we recommend reading the original Project Management Memory Jogger™ *and keeping it nearby while you read this book.*

Building the Project Management Infrastructure: Chapters 1 and 2

We start with building an organizational structure that supports and furthers project management success. We will look at:

✔ The importance of project sponsorship

✔ Three critical kinds of support for project managers

✔ How to adopt a project management methodology

✔ How to implement a project management office

✔ How to manage your product portfolio

Advanced Skills in Project Management: Chapters 3 through 7

We will continue by advancing and honing your skills in managing projects:

- ✔ How to tailor the amount of project management for your project
- ✔ How to define project success
- ✔ Ways to refine and control project scope
- ✔ Techniques for scheduling the work
- ✔ Five ways to manage project risk
- ✔ How to create baselines for, measure, control, and forecast project work

Leadership Skills for Project Managers and Team Members: Chapters 8 through 10

Experienced project managers need to master leadership skills as well as technical skills. With this in mind we will present information on:

- ✔ How to improve team communication
- ✔ Negotiation techniques
- ✔ Conflict resolution
- ✔ How to enhance your emotional intelligence
- ✔ How to choose a good leadership style
- ✔ Ways to ease organizational change
- ✔ Techniques for effective project team meetings

The chart below summarizes the topics you will likely be interested in, according to your role.

	Project Managers	Project Sponsors	Project Team Members and Subproject Team Leaders	Senior Managers and Project Executives *
	Project Manager	Project Sponsor	Team Member	Senior Mgmt
1. Building a Project Management Infrastructure	★	◉	★	◉
2. Managing Your Project and Program Portfolio	★	◉	★	◉
3. Tailoring Project Management to Your Project	◉	★	◉	★
4. Refining Your Project's Scope	◉	★	◉	★
5. Scheduling	◉	◉	◉	★
6. Managing Project Risk	◉	★	◉	★
7. Controlling Project Progress	◉	◉	◉	★
8. Improving Team Communication	◉	◉	◉	◉
9. Conducting Negotiations and Resolving Conflict	◉	◉	◉	★
10. Applying Effective Project Leadership	◉	◉	◉	◉

* Includes managers of project managers, project management office executives, and executives with accountability for projects or for project managers

◉ = Primary Interest   ★ = Secondary Interest

Chapter 1

Building a
Project Management
Infrastructure

To give your projects the best chance to succeed, your culture and environment need to support mature project management. Organizations that practice mature project management gain benefits such as shorter completion times, better control of costs, and improved customer satisfaction.

How can you describe and measure improved project performance across the organization? One way is to use a maturity model—specifically, a *project management maturity model*, or PMMM. The model defines four levels of maturity, describes each level, and outlines the expected results at each level.

Project Management Maturity Model

Maturity Level	Description	Expected Results
1. Informal	• Project managers manage projects in an ad hoc manner. • There is little accountability for project success. • There is no standard project management methodology. • There is no formal evaluation of the project portfolio. • There is no project office. • There is no commitment to improve the overall system.	• Unpredictable results • Intermittent success, dependent on the project manager's skills • Dissatisfied customers • Long cycle times

Continued on next page

Project Management Maturity Model (continued)

Maturity Level	Description	Expected Results
2. Standardized	• Project managers receive some project management training. • Sponsors write charters for the projects. • The organization follows a standard project management methodology. • The organization uses a common language and definitions. • The organization has one or more project offices. • The organization has a project portfolio steering committee. • The project portfolio steering committee defines the criteria for selecting and prioritizing projects.	• Pockets of improved results • Comparable results across different projects • Common terminology • An ability to define and measure project success • Developed best practices • Established methods of project selection
3. Core competency	• Project managers and team members have the skills needed to effectively manage projects. • Resource allocation matches resource availability. • All teams use a standard project management methodology and templates. • Project managers capture historical data and use it to improve performance. • The project office uses project metrics to measure project status. • The project portfolio steering committee selects and monitors all projects.	• Significantly improved performance across the organization • Increased project capacity • Reduced cycle times • Increased customer satisfaction • Increased efficiency and productivity • An optimized project portfolio
4. Continuous improvement	• The organization implements and measures ongoing improvement in technical processes, knowledge management, and project management. • The project management system is part of how the organization does business.	• Further reduced cycle times • Increased project capacity

The time and money you invest in improved project management pays off in improved project performance, which in turn enables the organization to meet its strategic goals and objectives faster, better, and more efficiently.

For an organization to advance beyond an informal maturity level, the executives must build a framework that supports project management. You don't need to know the details of managing projects, but you must provide an infrastructure that allows project management to grow and thrive.

You can create this infrastructure by taking four actions:

1. Create the role of a *project sponsor*. This person supports project managers (PMs) and acts as the liaison to senior management and/or the project steering committee.

2. Adopt a *project management methodology* that provides a standardized process for every project.

3. Implement a *project management office*. This office can serve many functions, including developing and maintaining the methodology, creating and maintaining templates and forms, mentoring project managers, and performing other key functions to support project success.

4. Create a *project portfolio management system*. Project portfolio management allows you to optimize your project selection and resource allocation and ensures that projects align with your strategic goals.

Note: We cover the first three actions in this chapter, and the fourth in Chapter 2.

The Project Sponsor

Except for very small projects, all projects should have a project sponsor (i.e., an executive who is accountable to the organization for the success of the project). A project sponsor is the liaison between the project, senior management, and the project portfolio steering committee. (More about this committee in the next chapter.)

The sponsor provides:

- Strategic input
- Management support
- Political assistance

These areas are generally outside of the project manager's area of influence, and by assuming these responsibilities, the project sponsor frees the project manager to focus on managing the project.

When you need to:	Check the section on:
Make decisions about the project in the overall organizational context	Providing strategic support to the project manager
Make decisions outside the project manager's realm of authority	Providing management support to the project manager
Assist in sensitive situations or those that require executive-level support	Providing political support to the project manager
Create a common method to plan and manage projects	Adopting a project management methodology
Manage the daily operations of all projects	Implementing project management offices

Providing Strategic Support to the Project Manager

Project Sponsor   Senior Mgmt

Why do it?

To ensure that the strategic goals of the organization are aligned and consistent with the tactical decisions made at the project level.

How do I do it?

1. **Determine the strategic priorities of the organization.**

   • Educate project managers about the thought processes behind strategic decisions so they can elevate their level of thinking.

2. **Make project decisions based on information about other initiatives.**

   • Use information about strategic priorities to rank multiple projects and set priorities in a given project. Adding a broader organizational perspective lets you create synergies between projects and helps prevent duplication.

3. **Monitor the project environment.**

   • Analyze the impact of future internal and external events that could affect the project, and make decisions that optimize the organization's position.

4. **Actively support the project.**

   • Having an active presence in the project encourages team members to perform well. It also communicates executive support for the project to functional managers, and enlists their cooperation.

Providing Management Support to the Project Manager

Why do it?

To provide the business case for the project, approve the project baselines (of scope, schedule, and cost), and approve major changes to the project.

How do I do it?

1. **When initiating a project, develop a business case to prove that the investment is prudent.**
   - Include:
     - An executive summary
     - A background explanation justifying the project
     - Market information
     - Financial models
     - A cost-benefit analysis or feasibility study
     - A risk and opportunity analysis
     - A recommended approach

2. **Create a charter for the project to give the project manager the authority to apply organizational resources.**
   - Include:
     - The justification for the project
     - The business need that the project meets
     - High-level deliverables
     - A rough budget or "not-to-exceed" limit
     - High-level milestones
     - High-level assumptions and constraints
     - Identified risks

The project charter identifies the project manager and delegates authority to him or her. If there are limitations on the project manager's authority (such as decisions on budgetary issues), you should also identify them in the charter.

Project charters are described in greater detail in the Project Management Memory Jogger™ *(PMMJ).*

3. **Approve the scope, schedule, and budget baselines.**

4. **Ensure that the project has sufficient resources (i.e., capital, people, and equipment).**

5. **Manage the "investments" for the project.**

   • Oversee the budget, and monitor spending at a high level to make certain that actual expenditures align with the budgeted expenditures throughout the project.

6. **Make decisions that are outside the authority of the project manager.**

   • Guide the project manager through complex or high-risk decisions.

7. **Manage conflicts with other projects.**

   • If conflicts arise between projects or between a project and a functional area outside of the project manager's authority or ability to resolve, assist in finding a resolution.

8. **Review the project's progress.**

   • Regularly review results at a high level. If there are unexpected results, have the project manager determine the root cause(s) and take appropriate action.

9. Review and approve significant changes to any of the project baselines.

10. Intervene in risk management as needed.
    • If an unforeseen event occurs that the project manager is not authorized to act on, work with him or her to develop an appropriate response.

11. Provide mentoring and coaching to the project manager.
    • When the project manager doesn't know the best approach for handling a situation, mentor and coach him or her to explore various options and select the best choice.

Providing Political Support to the Project Manager

Why do it?

To support the project and the project manager when politically savvy or high-level authority is needed to handle a situation.

How do I do it?

1. Resolve conflicts that the project manager brings to your attention.
   • Work with him or her to come up with alternatives to handle the conflict, or address the issue personally.

 If the conflict is with a higher-level executive, it is often best to have the sponsor handle the situation from the start.

©2006 GOAL/QPC

2. **Protect the project manager from organizational politics.**

   - When politically sensitive decisions need to be made, make them yourself and protect the project manager and the project team from having to get involved. This enables the project team to continue focusing on the project.
   - If there are internal conflicts at the management level, intervene to protect the project team from a potentially damaging situation.

Adopting a Project Management Methodology

Why do it?

To standardize the processes that project managers and project team members will follow. By requiring certain processes and procedures for each project, you will get more consistent outcomes.

 Who should implement a project management methodology? The best choice is either someone in the project management office or an executive in the organization who has responsibility for project management.

How do I do it?

1. **Define which processes, policies, procedures, and templates should be standardized, and which should remain at the discretion of the project manager.**

 When first introducing a methodology you may choose to make some processes mandatory, others discretionary, and still others optional, depending on the project's size and risk.

2. **Benchmark information on current internal practices, as well as best practices in the industry.**

   • Conduct research, hire external consultants, and take surveys, to collect this information.

3. **Write a methodology description and summary.**

   • Include intended outcomes, flowcharts, deliverables to be produced during each project phase, and a process for implementing the methodology.

4. **Develop forms, templates, examples, and other information that describes and defines the methodology.**

   • Include items such as a charter template, a sample of a completed risk analysis, or a sample change-request form.

   • Describe and explain each piece of the methodology, and develop guidelines that define when and how to use it.

5. **Roll out the methodology, and train all staff on its use.**

   • Set clear expectations regarding when and how to use the new methodology. You may choose to apply the new methodology only to new projects, or apply it immediately to all projects, even those now in execution. Make that decision by weighing the impact of projects that use the methodology against the extra work involved in bringing existing projects into compliance.

   Team members will adopt the methodology more quickly and outcomes will improve if you seek input from lead project managers. Getting advice on how best to adapt internal practices and adopt external practices ensures that the new approach is suited to your environment. It also gains buy-in from the most influential project managers.

6. Measure the results six months after implementation. Revise, refine, and update the methodology as needed.

Implementing Project Management Offices

The Project Management Institute defines a project management office (PMO) as "an organizational body or entity assigned various responsibilities related to the centralized and coordinated management of those projects under its domain." Project management offices—also called project offices (POs)—come in many shapes and sizes. The type of project management office your organization operates will be based on your needs. We describe five options below; however, your organization may be best served by a hybrid of these types.

Why do it?
To coordinate and manage the daily operations of all projects.

How do I do it?
1. From the tables of project management offices below, choose the most suitable one(s) for your organization.
   • You may wish to combine or eliminate some functions.

2. Set up the office and supply the needed resources.
   • Establish a business case to justify the project management office overhead costs.

- Seek out key stakeholders, define their project management office needs and wants, and enlist their support.
- Determine the office governance structure, including staffing, reporting, and authority.

3. **Implement the project office.**

Types of Project Management Offices

Type	Description	Provides or Includes:
Administrative Project Office	Serves as a repository for project management processes and paperwork	• Policies • Procedures • Forms • Methodology descriptions • Best practices
Project Support Office	Provides guidance and assists project managers and others in dealing with any kind of project issue	• Guidance for planning and launching major projects • Assistance for troubled projects • Mentoring and coaching • Assistance to non-managers who suddenly find themselves managing a project • Advice on anything to do with project management at any level of the organization
Center of Excellence	Collects and codifies best practices and seeks to improve project management throughout the organization. Combines some of the elements of administrative and support offices	• Policies and procedures • Forms and templates • Best practices • A repository for lessons learned • Benchmarking information • Methodology descriptions • Mentoring and coaching

Continued on next page

Types of Project Management Offices (continued)

Type	Description	Provides or Includes:
Center of Excellence (continued)		• Training and development for project managers • Expert advice on anything to do with project management at any level of the organization
Project Manager Business Unit	Is the business unit that project managers report to	• A reporting structure for project managers • Personal development • Project tools and procedures
Project-Specific Office	Is established for a specific project and disbanded when the project is complete	• Storage of all documentation for a specific project • Housing for most of the key personnel on the project team • Support for planning and monitoring the project

Here are the three most important things you can do to ensure the success of your project management office:

1. Clearly define the PMO's roles and responsibilities, and communicate them throughout the organization.

2. Be willing to make adjustments to meet organizational needs.

3. Give the system time to work.

Project Management Office Summary

Project Function	Administrative Office	Support Office	Center of Excellence	Business Unit	Project-Specific Office
Policies and procedures	✔		✔	✔	
Forms	✔		✔	✔	
Methodology	✔		✔	✔	
Best practices	✔		✔	✔	
Assistance for troubled projects		✔			
Mentoring and coaching		✔	✔	✔	
PM aid and assistance		✔			
Advice on project management throughout the organization		✔	✔		
Lessons-learned repository			✔		
Benchmarking information			✔		
Training for PMs			✔		
Certification programs			✔		
Functional home for PMs				✔	
Professional development			✔	✔	
Project-specific documentation					✔
Project-specific processes, forms, etc.					✔

Chapter 2

Managing Your Project and Program Portfolio

Most organizations reach a point where they have too many projects and not enough resources, and they can't efficiently schedule and manage the resources they have. They need a process to manage their portfolio of projects. This process has a number of benefits:

✔ It ensures that resources are available to the most important projects.

✔ It ensures that all projects support the strategic plan.

✔ It optimizes the project portfolio.

To implement project portfolio management, the first step is to establish a project portfolio steering committee (PPSC). Its role is to establish, maintain, and update the project and program portfolio.

A typical PPSC is composed of some or all of the following people:

- The director of the project management office

- A finance executive

- Operations executives

- Information technology (IT) executives

The needs of your organization will determine the specific makeup of the committee, but the members should come from the highest level of the organization to ensure that the portfolio is aligned with the organization's strategic vision.

Make sure that the project portfolio manager, as chair of the committee, reports directly to the CEO, the COO, or someone at that level of management.

Key Terms

Before we proceed, we should define some of the key terms we will use when discussing project and portfolio management. The following definitions are from the Third Edition of *A Guide to the Project Management Body of Knowledge* (the *PMBOK® Guide*; Project Management Institute, Newtown Square, PA).

Program: A group of related projects managed in a coordinated way to obtain benefits and control not available from managing them individually. Programs may include related work outside the scope of the discrete projects in the program.

Program management: The centralized, coordinated management of a program to achieve the program's strategic objectives and benefits.

Portfolio: A collection of projects or programs and other work that are grouped to facilitate effective management of that work to meet strategic business objectives. The projects or programs of the portfolio may not necessarily be interdependent or directly related.

Portfolio management: The centralized management of one or more portfolios, which includes identifying, prioritizing, authorizing, managing, and controlling projects, programs, and other related work, to achieve specific strategic business objectives.

©2006 GOAL/QPC

When you need to:	Check the section on:
List the existing projects in the organization	Identifying projects
Sort and group projects	Defining project categories
Find a method to select projects based on their merit to the organization	Developing project selection criteria
Rank existing projects against the selection criteria	Selecting and prioritizing projects
Make sure you have the right balance of projects in the portfolio	Finalizing the portfolio
Determine how well projects are performing	Monitoring project and portfolio performance
Add to, delete from, and rebalance the portfolio	Updating the portfolio

Identifying Projects

Why do it?

To determine the number and types of projects currently active in the organization and to document the "as is" state of affairs.

Note: This section assumes that a project portfolio manager has been identified and will be doing the work.

How do I do it?

1. **Collect the following information for all *current* projects in each division of the company:**
    - Project name
    - Project manager
    - Project duration
    - Project completion date
    - Project budget and the amount spent to-date
    - Estimated funds needed to complete the project
    - Number of full- and part-time team members by skill set
    - Reason for the project (e.g., benefits, business case, etc.)
    - Other related information (i.e., any interproject dependencies, risks of not completing the project, status, etc.)

2. **Gather the following information for all *proposed* projects in each division of the company:**
    - Project name
    - Estimated duration
    - Estimated budget range
    - Estimated number of full- and part-time team members by skill set
    - Reason for the project
    - Other related information (i.e., any interproject dependencies, risks of not completing the project, etc.)

3. **Compile the information on current and proposed projects into a list for use in the next section.**

**Sample List of Current
and Proposed Projects**

Current Projects

Project	Project Mgr	Justification	Estimated Duration	Estimated Finish	Estimated Budget	Resource Usage	Other
Introduce new functionality into product X	Derek	Increase market share. Stay competitive.	4 months	June	$95-105K ($35K spent to-date; estimated $65K still needed to complete the project)	3 full-time 5 part-time 1 contractor	Synergies with streamlining product Y
Decommission					$20-25K ($7K		

New Projects

Project	Justification	Estimated Duration	Estimated Finish	Estimated Budget	Resource Usage	Other
Streamline product Y	Increase market share. Increase profit margins on existing products.	4 months	July	$75-110K	4 full-time 2 part-time 1 consultant	Synergies with new functionality for product X
Place the manufacturing of components with an offshore company	Increase profit margins on existing products. Create operational efficiencies.	4 months	October	$35-55K	2 part-time 1 consultant	May impact turnaround time for new functionality in product X
Upgrade the data storage system	Create operational efficiencies.	4 months	December	$60-90K	2 full-time 4 part-time	

Defining Project Categories

Why do it?

To create a balanced project portfolio by determining a logical way to group and measure projects for selection and management.

How do I do it?

1. **Have the project portfolio steering committee review the list of current and proposed projects and look for logical ways to categorize them.**

   • Consider categorizing projects by:

   - Size

   - Risk level

   - Strategic objective

   - Market

   - Product line

   - Type (e.g., development, maintenance, etc.)

2. **Have the committee determine the weighting criteria for the project categories.**

   • Decide which projects have more importance than others. For example, you might decide that projects that provide a high return on investment are more important than those that increase market share or increase efficiency.

   • Define the right balance of projects for each category. Each organization will have different needs at different times, which will determine the correct balance of projects. An even spread might be appropriate, or some categories might have a higher allotment of projects than others.

©2006 GOAL/QPC

Categorized Project List

The Burkhardt Organization's strategic plan states that their primary objectives are, first, to increase their market share (objective A), then to increase their profit margin on existing projects (objective B) and finally, to find ways to create operational efficiencies (objective C).

After reviewing their strategic plan and list of potential new projects, the steering committee prioritized three new projects as follows:

Project	Meets Objective A	Meets Objective B	Meets Objective C	Priority
Introduce a streamlined version of our best-selling product	✔	✔		1
Place the manufacturing of component parts with an offshore company		✔		2
Upgrade the data storage system			✔	3

Developing Project Selection Criteria

Project Sponsor   Senior Mgmt

Why do it?

To ensure that only those projects that contribute to the organization are considered for addition to the portfolio.

Usually some type of financial criteria is included in the project selection criteria. You may choose to include other types of criteria (such as market factors, qualitative factors, and project-specific information) as well.

Even for qualitative categories, it is best to find a way to create a numeric weighting scale to minimize subjectivity. (Although subjective expert judgment can be useful in selecting projects when you cannot represent some factors in a scoring model, it's best to minimize your organization's dependence on this kind of subjectivity.)

How do I do it?

1. **Establish the screening criteria.**

   • Define the screening criteria for the project portfolio. Key considerations should include the organization's strategic plan, existing policies, and market projections.

   A project is "screened out" if it does not meet specific criteria, or "screened in" if it does meet the criteria.

   Some projects will automatically be screened in, such as those that have legal, regulatory, or compliance factors. Others that don't meet the strategic objectives of the organization or are in conflict with company policies will be screened out.

©2006 GOAL/QPC

2. Establish the weighting criteria.

- Define the quantitative and qualitative information you need to consider in selecting the best projects.

- Assign a weighted value to each category (i.e., a "category weight"). If appropriate, break each category into components and weight the components within the category (i.e., determine a "component weight") to create a scoring model.

- Define how you will assign scores for each of the components (i.e., what constitutes a score of 100, what constitutes a score of 90, etc.)

- Score each component of each category for each project.

- Multiply the score by the "component weight" for each component in each project. Sum these values to get a "category weight by project."

- Multiply the "category weight by project" by the "category weight" for each project, to get a "category score."

- Sum the scores by project to determine the project ranking.

Applying Project Weighting Criteria

Three projects are under consideration. (We assume that all of these projects have passed the initial screening criteria). The four weighting categories are financial considerations, market considerations, qualitative factors, and project factors. Each category has components. The components in each category total 100%, and the weighting for all categories totals 100%.

Continued on next page

Applying Project Weighting Criteria, continued

Weighting Categories and Components (A)	Category Weight (B)	Component Weight (C)	Project 1	Project 2	Project 3
Financial Considerations	30%				
Net present value		40%	80	25	75
Internal rate of return		20%	75	30	75 ⟩(D)
Payback period		40%	20	75	50
Category weight by proj.			*55*	*46*	*65* (E)
Market Considerations	30%				
Competition		25%	20	90	60
Penetration		25%	65	80	10
Market share		25%	60	85	10
New markets		25%	0	95	0
Category weight by proj.			*36.25*	*87.5*	*20*
Qualitative Factors	15%				
Synergies with other projects		50%	20	0	80
Ability to leverage in the future		20%	50	75	80
Strong internal support		30%	35	80	80
Category weight by proj.			*30.5*	*39*	*80*
Project Factors	25%				
Resource skills		20%	80	15	90
Resource availability		25%	80	20	60
Technology (realistic and available)		25%	80	20	100
Risk level		10%	70	20	90
Dependencies with other projects		10%	10	15	90
Operations support after implementation		10%	65	10	100
Category weight by proj.			*70.5*	*17.5*	*8.6*

Continued on next page

Applying Project Weighting Criteria, continued

Weighting Categories and Components (A)	Category Weight (B)	Component Weight (C)	Project 1	Project 2	Project 3
Category Scores					
Financial score	**30%**		16.5	13.8	19.5
Market score	**30%**		10.875	26.25	6.0
Qualitative score	**15%**		4.575	5.85	12.0 (F)
Project score	**25%**		17.625	4.4	21.5
Total Score			49.575	50.3	59 (G)

*For the sake of simplicity we did not explicitly define how the scoring was derived for each component. You will base this score on your organizational priorities.

(A) Quantitative/qualitative information to consider

(B) Category weight

(C) Component weight

(D) Component score

(E) Category weight by project

(F) Category score

(G) Project score

As you can see, project 3 scores highest and is the best selection, given the selection criteria.

Selecting and Prioritizing Projects

Why do it?

To apply objective, agreed-to selection criteria in determining which projects should continue, which should be eliminated, and which new ones should be initiated.

How do I do it?

1. Have the PPSC put the list of existing projects through the project screening criteria, rejecting any that fail.

2. Assess and rank the existing projects via the weighting criteria.

3. Put the list of proposed projects through the screening criteria, dismissing any that fail.

4. Put the proposed projects through the weighting criteria and rank the proposed projects according to the criteria.

The final result will be two lists of prioritized projects: those that are currently in progress and those that are proposed. You may also have a list of canceled and unapproved projects. Once you have a numerical ranking of the projects, you should always give it a final review. The quantitative results don't always take into consideration project synergies, resource constraints, or other qualitative factors.

©2006 GOAL/QPC

Finalizing the Portfolio

Why do it?

To determine whether resources exist to support all current and new projects.

How do I do it?

1. **Place the prioritized existing projects into categories established by the PPSC.**

   • Use project categories such as new product development, infrastructure development, and maintenance projects.

   • Establish guidelines for the percentage of projects (or dollars) that should be active in each category at any given time.

2. **Determine whether any categories exceed the established weighting allocation.**

   • If any of the categories have more projects than the weighting allocation allows, use the ranking system to determine which projects to postpone.

   • If some categories are underrepresented, add projects from the list of prioritized proposed projects.

3. **Assess the projects and categories until you find the "right mix."**

   • The right mix is the one that is closest to the balance you established when you defined your project categories (in step 2 of the "Defining Project Categories" section of this chapter).

Note: You won't be able to balance your projects perfectly, but you should work to come reasonably close.

Monitoring Project and Portfolio Performance

Why do it?

To ensure that the established categories, criteria, and overall performance are proceeding as planned, and to take preventive or corrective action if needed.

How do I do it?

1. **Review project performance using the project status reports provided by the project managers.**

   • At a minimum, these reports should include:

     - Project milestone performance

     - Project cost performance

     - High risks

2. **Establish control limits so that you manage project performance by exception (i.e., conduct detailed reviews only for those projects that are running behind or that have exceeded the preestablished budget variance).**

   • Address any risks that have surfaced that have a high impact, as well as risks that have a high probability and a medium impact. (Risk is addressed in greater detail in Chapter 6.)

3. **Periodically assess project information by category to detect any trends in performance.**

   • Investigate any schedule or cost trends in a portfolio category by determining the root cause(s).

   • Find ways to mitigate the impact of cost or schedule variances.

4. **Periodically assess project information by category to see whether the portfolio is performing to expectations.**

   • Determine whether the current balance of categories is appropriate.

   • Reassess whether the screening and weighting criteria are appropriate.

   • Initiate any changes necessary to achieve the performance goals of the portfolio.

Updating the Portfolio

Why do it?

To keep your portfolio balanced by closing completed projects and initiating new ones.

How do I do it?

1. **During project portfolio steering committee meetings, note any projects that have been completed.**

   • Delete the completed projects from the portfolio list.

2. **Select the highest scoring project (based on the weighting criteria) in the appropriate category from the list of approved potential projects.**

   • Add the highest scoring project to the portfolio.

3. **Review the portfolio to see whether it is in balance, as per the preestablished criteria.**

   • If it is not in balance, either adjust the current projects or add approved new projects.

Chapter 3

Tailoring Project Management
to Your Project

So far we've looked at projects from the point of view
of the larger organization. Now it's time to look at the
other side of the mirror: finding a place for the individual
project within the business framework. How do you get
the financial and other support you need from management to make the project a success? For that matter, how
will you, your customers, and your organization define
what "success" means for your particular project? And
how do you know what support you will need?

If this sounds confusing—you have to do "A" before
you can do "B," and you have to do "B" before you can
do "A"—that's because it is. The process of adapting
project management to your project is an *iterative* one.
You find out what your customers want, you work with
them and with the organization to define success for your
project, and then you assess what you'll need to meet
that definition. Then you work to adjust each piece of the
puzzle—customer requirements, business requirements,
and the needed support—until you have adapted your
project management approach to fit the facts.

> *This is early in the project—preplanning. You'll
> do a thorough risk analysis and detailed scope
> definition later during planning.*
>
> *Projects that succeed without any project manage-
> ment, if they actually exist, are a happy accident*

Continued on next page

> *or the result of an extremely talented project team.*
> *Large, complex projects need a great deal of project*
> *management. Small, simple projects do not need*
> *as much detail, but they still need project manage-*
> *ment. Your challenge is to find the right balance.*

When you need to:	Check the section on:
Find out what the project needs to accomplish for its customers	Determining your customers' needs
Discover what your organization expects and manage those expectations	Defining success for your project
Make preliminary assessments of what kind and how much project management your project needs	Adapting project management to your project

Determining Your Customers' Needs

Why do it?

To find out what the project needs to accomplish for its customers.

How do I do it?

1. **Review the charter and other documentation you have.**

   • Have a conversation with the project sponsor (face to face, if possible) to determine if there have been any changes that will affect your project, and to verify your understanding of key players and deliverables.

2. **During the project's planning stage, determine how your customers and sponsor will define success for the project.**

   • Hold discussions and meetings as necessary to elicit requirements and acceptance criteria.

3. **In addition to requirements for the product or service, identify things (such as any support services) that you are to provide.**

   • Be sure to include any organizational deliverables.

Defining Success for Your Project

Why do it?

To discover and manage your organization's expectations.

How do I do it?

1. **Working with your team, discuss the relative complexity, risk, and uncertainty of your project, based on:**

   • The experience of your team in doing the work

   • The technology you're using

   • The available resources

   • The organizational acceptance and understanding of the project

   • The technical process(es) to produce the project's deliverables

2. **Assign a number from 1 to 6 to represent the project's relative complexity and uniqueness.**

- For example, a rating of 1 may mean a project of this type has never been done by your team, or the technology may be new, unproven, or perhaps never used in this way.

A rating of 1 is like putting astronauts on Mars— a highly challenging effort (at least, as of this writing). A rating of 6 is like mass-producing cars on an assembly line or processing credit card transactions—a familiar process that has been repeated many times before and improved.

3. **Have this same discussion with your project sponsor and other executives, and ask them to rate the project in the same way.**

   - Executives and managers often underestimate how challenging a project is, because they are steeped in the operations end of things.

4. **When you have discussed the ratings with management and your team, determine whether there is a difference in how leadership sees the project and how you and your team see it.**

   - If your project rating (truth) is different from management's project rating (perception), then educate management on the reality of the project—especially if it is riskier and less efficient than they anticipate.

The actual numbers you get aren't very important. What is important is the gap between your expectations and those of management. The 1–6 scale is a guide to describe how challenging the project will be and a test to see whether you and management are in agreement. It is an intu-

Continued on next page

itive, early "guesstimate" of your project's complexity and challenges, based on high-level information (not a detailed analysis) at this point.

As you define the project success criteria, also account for the needs of team members. (You could even ask them what is important to them.) It is not pleasant to work on a project that the team believes can't be successful. Team members should have a chance to grow and develop new skills from their work on the project.

Educating Management About Your Project

To educate management about your project, you need to understand why managers think the way they do.

According to the *PMBOK® Guide*, a project is a "temporary endeavor undertaken to create a unique product, service, or result." Project management, then, is "the application of knowledge, skills, tools, and techniques to project activities to meet project requirements." Projects, in short, are the way organizations implement their strategic plans and create and improve new products, services, and processes.

This is in contrast to regular business operations, which are "business as usual"—the repetitive daily tasks that create or support the products and services offered by an organization to its customers. Business operations have a strong and proven infrastructure (i.e., job descriptions, organizational charts, procedures, etc.). (Note: Unless you have a strong project management office, this type of support may not exist for projects.)

Continued on next page

How Projects Differ from Operations

Projects	Business Processes or Operations
• Temporary; one-of-a-kind	• Permanent; mass-produced
• Unique output	• Repetitive output
• No preassigned jobs	• Job descriptions and assignments
• For many projects, the processes that produce the deliverables must be created.	• The deliverables process and technical processes are clearly defined, documented, refined, and continuously improved.
• Different inputs each time	• The same inputs or supplies each time
• Not part of the permanent structure of the organization and may not be part of the annual performance evaluation of individuals	• Part of the permanent structure of the organization and part of the annual performance evaluation of individuals
• May require the development of a project management methodology	• Part of a periodic planning cycle and standard process
• Project duties may not be part of each individual's performance evaluation and compensation, and may interfere with performance ratings.	• Job duties are the basis for each individual's performance evaluation and compensation.

These differences explain why projects tend to be riskier and less efficient than regular business operations, and why many business managers have unrealistic expectations for projects. They are more familiar with operations, where risks tend to be lower and more predictable, efficiency is higher, and rework is lower.

Continued on next page

Additionally, organizations earn revenue through normal business operations, but the benefits of projects, including any increases in revenue, lie in the future. Thus, when a project needs resources, support, or priority, managers may view it as a drain on human resources and an interference with business operations. The organization doesn't immediately feel the consequences of denying or delaying resources to a project.

If management decides to delay your project, quantify the impact in time and money (money is the language of business) that the delay will have. For example, take the number of days or weeks delayed and multiply it by the project's expected increase in profit or savings per time period.

Many people assume that if they deliver the project on time and within budget and if the customer accepts it, they have done their job well. But a good project manager also makes sure that the project meets the organization's needs as well. (Perhaps the project team members developed new, more-efficient ways of operating that can be documented as best practices.) Be sure to ask what additional benefits are expected of the project.

Factors Affecting the Ability
of Projects to Succeed

- *More projects.* For many organizations, the increasing pace of business, shortened product life cycles, global competition, and the need for nimbleness and flexibility result in the need to launch more and smaller projects.

- *Poor estimates of project effort.* Many organizations underestimate the complexity and size of projects—especially those projects that are not well-defined—or misunderstand their impact on the organization.

- *Conflicts with operations over resources.* Project work suffers if team members also have organizational responsibilities vital to the success of the business. When there is a conflict between project work and operations work, companies often defer project work, resulting in project delays or requiring additional effort by the project manager to stay on schedule.

Adapting Project Management to Your Project

Why do it?

To make preliminary assessments of what kind and how much management your project needs.

How do I do it?

1. **Review, with your team members, the results of the exercise you did earlier (when you rated your project on a scale of 1 to 6 in terms of its relative complexity, risk, and uniqueness).**

   • Use this data, as well as your intuition, to analyze the project's risk and complexity.

   • Inform the project sponsor, project executives, and senior management that these and other factors could prevent the team from meeting the organization's definition of project success.

2. **Conduct a high-level, preliminary risk analysis to determine how much planning, controlling, and monitoring your project will need.**

   • For example, suppose there is a strong chance of missing a project deadline. You have a few options: you can add activities to prevent the delay, you can monitor the work more closely, or you can both monitor the work *and* add activities. (With the third option, you will know whether your dates are at risk and can get back on track before it is too late.)

    This risk analysis is intended to be intuitive and preliminary. For a more-formal risk analysis, see Chapter 6.

3. **Brainstorm ideas to minimize risks and improve efficiency.**

   • Audit the infrastructure. In many organizations, the processes and infrastructure to support projects are minimal or nonexistent. (In contrast, the infrastructure available to support business

---

operations includes well-developed lean processes, predictable risks and outputs, experienced people, higher efficiency, and less rework.) Determine how your team can access or create the infrastructure that the project needs.

> *If you have a project management office, it may be easier to find out what assistance is available than if the subject of project support has not yet been addressed. You'll need to know which support services your project will need and which ones are available and suitable. For example, are you using scheduling software, and will there be someone to input and update it? Do planning and reporting templates currently exist, and are they suitable for your project "as is" or do they require modification?*

4. **Determine the level of project management that your project will require and how much detail and analysis is needed.**

   • In addition to the factors you considered in step 2, look at:

     - The number of deliverables conveyed from one individual or subproject to another

     - The number of people and organizations involved

     - The number of locations or sites

Here's a handy summary that shows how the level of project management affects project attributes.

Project Attribute	More Project Management (Large, Critical, or Complex Projects)	Less Project Management (Small, Simple Projects)
Schedule	Schedule contains milestone dates, interdependencies of deliverables, and detailed activities.	Schedule contains only milestone dates.
Cost budget	Cost estimates contain detailed estimates both of internal costs (i.e., employee labor costs, internal charges) and external costs (i.e., subcontracts and purchase orders).	Cost estimate is not itemized.
Staff effort budget	Labor budget contains detailed estimates of effort hours by activity.	Labor estimate is a single, imprecise number based on past experience or the number of people and duration of tasks.
Risk analysis	Risk analysis is always current and contains probabilities and impact or decision-tree calculations, along with risk triggers and budget and schedule contingencies.	Risk analysis contains a brief list of the risks and planned responses or countermeasures.
Communications	Communications involve an elaborate communications plan (who, what, how, and when).	Communications include a basic communications plan or status report.
Scope	Scope is fully developed, and all deliverables are adequately defined.	Scope is limited to a list of deliverables with acceptance criteria.
Procurement	Procurement plan contains a list of planned subcontracts and purchase orders, including costs and lead times, expediting, and quality assurance plans.	Procured items are included in the cost estimates and schedule dates. There is no separate procurement plan.
Project controls	Status reports include risk, cost, schedule, effort, issues, and earned value analysis.	Status reports include actual completion dates, costs and effort, and issues.

Tailoring Project Management 41

Remember that tailoring project management to your project is an iterative process. You may need to repeat steps as you acquire more information and refine your understanding.

An excellent rule of thumb is to include the following project management elements in all projects (to the level that you, as the person accountable for the success of the project, feel comfortable with):

- *Deliverables and acceptance criteria*
- *Schedule*
- *Cost estimate*
- *Staff effort estimate*
- *Risk analysis*

Chapter 4

Refining Your Project's Scope

The first step in building a credible project management plan is to define the scope of your project. For your project to be successful, the deliverables must satisfy your customers' wants and needs, also known as their *requirements*. If you don't accurately define and document the project scope, the project won't satisfy the customers' requirements—even if it is on time and within budget.

As discussed in the *Project Management Memory Jogger*™, defining the project scope involves four steps:

1. Expanding on the project scope description.

2. Determining what interim deliverables need to be produced.

3. Determining what processes and other projects fall within the scope of your project.

4. Creating a tree diagram of subprojects and work assignments (i.e., a work breakdown structure).

> *Remember: a* deliverable *is a product, service, or process; a* final deliverable *is what is delivered to the customers of the project, and an* interim deliverable *is produced during the creation of the final deliverable.*
>
> *An* operational deliverable *reflects the business results the organization expects from*
>
> Continued on next page

the project (i.e., the benefits to the organization—a 4% increase in market share or a 3-point improvement in customer satisfaction ratings—that the business owner will realize at some time after the project is over). The project team cannot be held accountable for operational results because they are outside the project team's control and will be realized in the future. Project success should be judged by the project's final deliverables *(e.g., an improved new product development process or an updated database) that the project customer will use to obtain the business results after the project is over.*

When you need to:	Check the section on:
Understand the customers' requirements	Creating a deliverables table
Organize the deliverables	Elaborating the work breakdown structure
Analyze changes in more depth	Controlling project scope changes

Creating a Deliverables Table

Why do it?

To ensure that your project deliverables satisfy customers' and stakeholders' expectations and that the product has the required capability, conditions, features, and functions.

The Deliverables Table

A *deliverables table* summarizes the project's deliverables and other relevant information. The template below captures customer needs, prioritized customer requirements (features and functions), and detailed customer acceptance criteria.

Deliverables Table

Attribute	Description	Deliverable 1	Deliverable 2	Deliverable n
Deliverable	Name the deliverable (final or interim).			
Authorization	Write the name of the individual who represents the users and has authority to sign off on the deliverable. (The project customer and the user may be the same person or entity.)			
Customer requirements (Features and functions)	Describe what the customer has asked for. Explain why the deliverable is needed, and rank its priority. List the features and functions of the final deliverable.			
Customer acceptance criteria	List the criteria the customer will use to define satisfaction. (Make sure these criteria are fully understood and agreed to.)			

How do I do it?

1. **Populate a deliverables table with information on the project's scope.**

- Review the scope section of the project charter and the results of the scope planning you have completed so far.

2. **Identify the project's customers and the authority that each has.**

   - Determine who can approve budgets, make changes to acceptance criteria, and modify requirements. In complex projects, there may be multiple customers; be sure to clarify exactly which function or area each one controls.

   A customer table can help you capture this information. To start, have the team members brainstorm all of the project's customers and stakeholders, then list their requirements.

   Not all projects need a customer table and some projects may have more customers than the three basic ones listed in the example below. If you have multiple customers and conflicting requirements, you will need to convene a meeting to resolve any differences.

Customer Table

Customer or Functional Role*	Asks the Question:	Customer Role Approves or Disapproves:	Accountable Individual	Requirements
Economic or financial	Is it worth the investment?	Expenditures	(Name of authorizing individual)	
Technical	Does it meet the technical specifications? Will it work?	Technical issues	(Name of authorizing individual)	
User	Will it do what I need it to do?	Functionality or user interface	(Name of authorizing individual)	

* One person may fill one or more of these roles, and you may have additional roles.

3. **Review the deliverables table with customers and/or users.**

   • Capture their requirements, comments, clarifications, and changes.

   • Note: Users are project customer(s) or are represented by the project customer(s).

4. **Translate customer and stakeholder requirements into the features and functions of the deliverables.**

   • Determine how each requirement will be met by the features and functions.

   • Map each requirement to a deliverable, and assign accountability for creating each deliverable.

5. **Finalize the acceptance criteria for each deliverable.**

   • Work with your team to determine whether each criterion you have developed is "SMART":

S	Specific	• Can be understood only one way • Free of ambiguities and unverifiable terms • Stated positively
M	Measurable	• Can be verified
A	Achievable	• Can be done within project constraints
R	Realistic	• Makes sense • Is appropriate for the requirement
T	Tangible	• Stated in numerical form or yes/no format, or in accordance with an established, understood, and recognized definition, procedure, or standard

   If you don't have all of the information to answer these questions, either stop to collect the information, or determine if the answer to the question is necessary for success.

Be sure to involve the project customers as well as the project team in this effort. You'll get more accurate information and buy-in for the project.

 For a more sophisticated analysis of software requirements, see The Software Requirements Memory Jogger™ *(GOAL/QPC, Salem, NH).*

Elaborating the Work Breakdown Structure

The Work Breakdown Structure: Subproject Tree Format

If your project has more than a few deliverables, you have probably already planned to use the subproject tree diagram in the *Project Management Memory Jogger™* (also called a *work breakdown structure,* or *WBS*). A WBS organizes and defines the total scope of the project as deliverables, which are grouped to align with the way the work will be performed and controlled.

Your WBS is the foundation of your *project management plan,* which contains the project schedule, a risk assessment, the team composition, and other information. The project management plan includes information on the project deliverables, designates accountability for the deliverables, and describes the organizational structure of the project team.

Continued on next page

A Work Breakdown Structure for a 3-Day Conference

Level 1	Level 2: Subprojects and Person Accountable	Level 3: Subproject Final Deliverables
Project: 3-Day Conference	**Project Management** Amy Lee (Project Manager)	Process Evaluation Report Conference Plan
	Facilities Jose Ferrara (Subproject Leader)	Hotel/Food Contracts Conference Tapes Audiovisual Equipment Facilities Coordination
	Registrations Linda Saunders (Subproject Leader)	Marketing Information Booth Materials Registered Participants Registration List
	Program Development Amy Lee (Subproject Leader)	Internal Presentations External Presentations Program Proceedings Conference Guide
	Marketing Andy Wellman (Subproject Leader)	Brochure Postcard

Why do it?

To define your project scope according to the deliverables and then group the deliverables in an efficient, effective way.

How do I do it?

1. **Define the subprojects.**

    • Determine how to organize the work of the project. The top level of the WBS (level 1) is the name of the project. The next level down (level 2) shows the subproject names—how the project will be organized—and the name of the subproject leader. Level 3 begins with the major deliverables of the project, which are usually the final deliverables of the subprojects, and these are further decomposed as interim deliverables.

> *Most projects are divided into subprojects according to functional areas or work groups but you shouldn't assume that the subprojects are always organized this way, even if your organization itself is so structured. Subprojects can also be broken down by:*
>
> • *Geography*
>
> • *Region*
>
> • *Product line*
>
> • *Customer*
>
> • *Industry*
>
> • *Calendar*
>
> • *Business unit*
>
> • *Work process*
>
> • *Functional area*

Continued on next page

Breaking down the work is a strategic decision. A good choice may enhance coordination of the work and minimize political issues.

Don't forget to include a subproject for "project management." Managing a project creates its own deliverables, and if the project's final deliverable requires integration, it may be done by the project manager.

2. **Verify the final deliverables, subproject leaders, and corresponding acceptance criteria for each subproject and deliverable.**

3. **Map the interim deliverables to the subprojects until you have enough information to plan the work.**

4. **Have the subproject leader assign someone from the subproject team to each deliverable.**

   • Have the subproject leader, the accountable person, and the subproject team estimate the duration and cost of each deliverable or subproject at a high level.

Estimating the duration and budget for each deliverable is always a good idea, but some organizations do not support nor require all of this information. Effective project managers estimate it anyway to help them better manage the project. (See the Project Management Memory Jogger™ *for more information on estimating.)*

Elaborating the WBS is an iterative process. At first you may have only three levels, with rough estimates of time and cost. After decomposing the work and creating a detailed schedule and budgets, you can add that detail to the WBS.

Controlling Project Scope Changes

Why do it?

To understand the reasons for changes in the project's scope and thus plan for and better control them.

How do I do it?

1. **When a change is proposed, decide whether or not it is a good idea.**

   • Requests for changes may come from someone outside of the team, such as the sponsor or a customer. Also, as team members are monitoring any changes in the environment, they may need to propose changes that will address a problem that has occurred or has the potential to occur. Changes in the environment can include organizational, regulatory, competitive, and technological changes that could have an impact on the project.

   Not every proposed change should be adopted. Be sure to ask, "Is this change good for the customer? The organization? The project?"

   • If the change will not add value to the project, put it on an issues list to resolve with the person who requested the change. (Refer to the *Project Management Memory Jogger™* for more information on issues lists.)

2. **If the change is a good idea and doesn't require modifying the project management plan, implement the change.**

   • If the change doesn't modify the project scope, customer acceptance criteria, schedule, staff time, budget, or risk level of the project, implement it but be sure to document the change as a clarification of the project.

3. **If the change requires modifying the project management plan, define the impact on the plan and prepare a change order.**
   * A change order is a one-page description of the proposed change and its impact on the project (i.e., How will the change affect the risk level of the project? The cost? The schedule?).

Change Order

Date: 7/10   **Originator:** Amy Lee
Change order number: 15

Description of change: Go to an outside printer to print conference proceedings instead of printing in house

Why needed: Our in-house print shop has difficulty meeting deadlines because equipment reliability is low and the projected workload in August is high, putting a strain on the operation

Change requested: Go to an outside printer

Proposed solution: Request bids and print proceedings with an outside supplier

Impact on project scope: None

Risk rating for the conference: Improved

Impact on team: None

Impact on deadline dates: No impact if the change order is approved

Risk ratings for deadline dates: Improved

Impact on budget: $500 increase

Impact on project reports: None

Date approved:

| _____ | _____ | _____ |
| Project Leader | Sponsor | Customer |

- Most parts of the project management plan are interdependent, meaning that if one part of the plan is changed, other parts will likely need to be changed as well. For example, if a change to the project scope is required, it will probably affect the schedule, staff time, budget, risks of creating the deliverables, and reviews and approvals needed. Be sure the team examines all of the ramifications of a requested change.

> *A change to the project management plan is really a mini-project; therefore, the team needs to follow the same set of steps that it did to create its original project management plan. However, if the changes are simple, the team can go through the steps quickly.*
>
> *Let the priorities of the project guide the team in deciding how to modify the project management plan. For example, if the schedule is most important and a change has been requested to the scope of the project, look for ways to change the staff time and budget before modifying the schedule.*

4. **Have the change order approved, and implement the change.**

- Usually the project leader and the sponsor approve the change order. You should also have customers approve the change order if the change will affect them or if they will also approve the budget and/or scope.

---

5. **Update the project management plan to incorporate the change.**
   • It is the project leader's responsibility to incorporate the change by amending the appropriate parts of the project management plan.

Five Common Reasons for a Project's Scope Change

1. Errors in defining the deliverables, including missing, unnecessary, or inaccurate deliverables.

2. Errors in defining the project. The deliverables are correct, but the project was incorrectly defined in the first place.

3. Customer or stakeholder requests. To minimize unnecessary changes in project scope, early in the project, you should define and publish the criteria and the timeline for accepting discretionary project scope changes.

4. Value-added changes. For example, a team member may find a better, faster, less-expensive way to do the work and still meet the project objectives.

5. External events. These types of changes—changes in regulatory requirements, changes in the organization's priorities, or changes in the market or technology—are outside of

Continued on next page

Refining Your Project's Scope 55

the project manager's control but must still be accommodated.

Chapter 5

Scheduling

Although a schedule may have multiple or parallel branches of the same length, every project schedule has one *critical path* (i.e., the longest path through the schedule and the shortest time to complete the project). Deliverables on the critical path *must be completed by their late finish dates (explained below) for the project to be completed as scheduled.* If the completion date of any deliverable on the critical path is delayed, the project completion date will also be delayed, unless changes (to duration, resources, and/or scope) are made.

(Note: For simplicity's sake, we will use the word "deliverable" when referring to items on the project schedule or WBS. "Deliverable" may refer to an activity, task, interim deliverable, subdeliverable, or final deliverable.)

You must focus on the parts of your schedule that can delay project completion, and allocate sufficient resources to these critical items. When schedule problems occur, you can manage the critical path to help resolve your schedule issues and stay on track.

Key Scheduling Terms

Reserve: an amount of money or time that you allow above the estimates in the project management plan; it may also be called management reserve or contingency reserve. Having a contingency reserve reduces the risk of not meeting project objectives. (For more on managing project risks, see Chapter 6.)

Critical deliverable: a deliverable that must be completed on schedule for the project to finish on time. A critical deliverable has zero float—the early start and finish dates are the same as the late start and finish dates.

Predecessor: a deliverable that must start or finish before another deliverable can start or finish.

Successor: a deliverable that follows a predecessor.

Early start (ES) date: the earliest date that a deliverable can start, based on the early finish dates of predecessor deliverables.

Early finish (EF) date: the earliest date that a deliverable can finish, based on its duration and early start date.

Late start (LS) date: the latest date that a deliverable can start without delaying the project end date, based on the late finish dates of predecessor deliverables.

Late finish (LF) date: the latest date that a deliverable can finish without delaying the project end date, based on its duration and late start date.

Total float: the total amount of time that the early start date of a deliverable can be delayed without delaying the project finish date; it is the difference

Continued on next page

between the project's early finish and late finish dates, and may simply be called "float."

Free float: the amount of time that a deliverable can be delayed without delaying the early start of any immediately following deliverables.

Duration: the amount of time on a calendar (usually a number of working hours, days, or weeks) that you estimate and allocate to complete a deliverable.

Effort: the number of staff hours, days, weeks, or labor units required to complete a deliverable.

Network: a schematic diagram of the logical relationships among project deliverables; it is also called a project schedule network diagram.

Overallocation: the scheduling of resources to do more work than can be accomplished in the specified time.

When you need to:	Check the section on:
Know what you need before you start	Getting started
Develop the schedule for producing the project's deliverables	Creating the deliverables schedule
Develop and manage schedule contingency	Determining schedule contingency
Ensure that the schedule is valid	Establishing a valid schedule baseline
Manage the schedule to stay or get back on track	Managing the project schedule during execution

Getting Started

Why do it?

To launch your project successfully and efficiently.

 If you completed a deliverables table (in Chapter 4), you will find much of the information you need to start scheduling your project there.

How do I do it?

1. **Gather the information you've prepared about the project's scope.**

   • As project manager, you have met with your core team members and subproject leaders to develop a WBS for your project (see the *Project Management Memory Jogger*™ and Chapter 4 of this book), so you will already have:

     - A work breakdown structure, which defines the subproject organization

     - A final list of project and subproject deliverables (final and interim)

     - An initial list of the people accountable for the work of each subproject and deliverable

     - Initial acceptance criteria for the final and interim project and subproject deliverables that are critical or at risk for rework or delays

2. **Have each subproject leader/core team member work with their team to develop the details of the deliverables they are responsible for.**

- Write each deliverable on a sticky note for use in creating the project's deliverables schedule (explained in the next section of this chapter). These details, as needed for each deliverable, include:
  - The predecessor(s) for each deliverable
  - The name of the person (or people) accountable to create the deliverables or perform the activities

3. **Estimate the duration of each deliverable and include it on the sticky note.**
  - Be sure to consider:
    - The estimated effort to complete the deliverable
    - The risks associated with the deliverable (which increase uncertainty)
    - An allowance for waiting for comments or other information
    - Contingency time for risks

> *You may not yet have all of this information but the process of building your schedule will allow your team to collaborate and negotiate.*
>
> Always *have team members take part in developing this information so that they believe it is both accurate and achievable; you'll need their support to execute the project. If you have been following good project management practices, you will have already developed most of this information during scope planning. If you don't have it, stop and refer to the* Project Management Memory Jogger™ *for an explanation and details on how to do this with your team.*

Analogous estimating: Compare the project to similar previous projects.

Parametric estimating: Use standard rates as a guide.

Three-point estimating: Average the optimistic, most likely, and pessimistic estimates for the deliverable into one score.

Using resources: Divide the number of effort hours by the number of available hours per time period. For example, if a deliverable is estimated to take 160 hours and you have two people working a total of 80 hours per week, the duration should be at least two weeks.

Be sure to consider risks, productivity levels, and the accuracy of the estimates, and use expert judgment to finalize durations.

4. **Determine the types of schedules you will need.**

   • Consider these questions:

     - Do you need to further define the activities required to complete each deliverable?

     - Does your team have experience in a project of this type?

     - Are the project risks high?

     - Are the times allowed for completing the deliverables adequate given the acceptance criteria?

     - Does the team feel the schedule is achievable?

Your project may require different types of schedules. For example, you may need a milestone schedule to show important dates to the project sponsor, the project portfolio steering committee, and key stakeholders. In addition to a milestone schedule, your project may need a deliverables schedule to show customers the project's interim and final deliverables and interdependencies. You may also need an activity schedule to help your team track the execution of the project.

Schedule Types

Type	Purpose of This Schedule
Milestone schedule	To communicate the planned dates of major milestones to the sponsor, stakeholders, or customers at a high level. (Note: Every project needs a milestone schedule. It may provide enough planning for your project, or you may need additional schedules.)
Deliverables schedule	To define the sequence and predecessors of your project deliverables (similar to a flowchart of the project's work, organized by subprojects).
Activity schedule	To break the deliverables into subproject activities showing who is doing what and when. Used for tracking and execution, it should be more precise than the deliverables schedule.

A Milestone Schedule for a 3-Day Conference

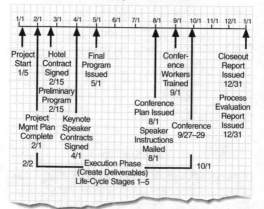

Project Start 1/5
Hotel Contract Signed 2/15
Preliminary Program 2/15
Final Program Issued 5/1
Conference Workers Trained 9/1
Closeout Report Issued 12/31
Process Evaluation Report Issued 12/31

Project Mgmt Plan Complete 2/1
Keynote Speaker Contracts Signed 4/1
Conference Plan Issued 8/1
Speaker Instructions Mailed 8/1
Conference 9/27–29

2/2 — Execution Phase (Create Deliverables) Life-Cycle Stages 1–5 — 10/1

A Partial Deliverables Schedule for a 3-Day Conference

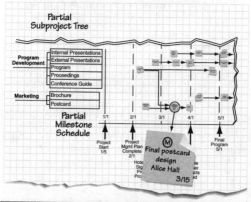

Partial Subproject Tree

Program Development
- Internal Presentations
- External Presentations
- Program
- Proceedings
- Conference Guide

Marketing
- Brochure
- Postcard

Partial Milestone Schedule

Project Start 1/5
Project Mgmt Plan Complete 2/1
Final Program 5/1

Hotel Signed Pro...
...er ...cts ...ed

(M) Final postcard design Alice Hall 3/15

A Partial Activity Schedule for a 3-Day Conference

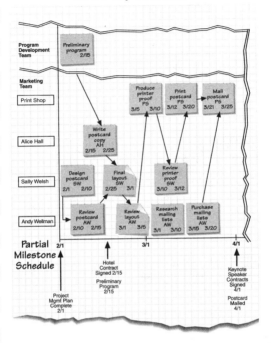

Note: All dates shown are in North American (month/day) format. For example, the date is "1/5" is January 5th.

Creating the Deliverables Schedule

Why do it?

To create an interdependent schedule that is easy for stakeholders to understand.

> *The deliverables schedule is the logical flow of the work; think of it as a flowchart with dates.*

How do I do it?

1. Working with the core team/subproject leaders, create a deliverables schedule diagram using the deliverables sticky notes you created in the previous section.

   • Hang four to five pieces of flipchart paper on a table or a wall. Place milestone dates on sticky notes across the bottom (the x-axis), and list the subprojects down the left side (the y-axis).

> *Don't forget to include a subproject named "project management."*

Sticky Notes vs. Scheduling Software

When a team cannot be in the same room and use sticky notes, it is often helpful to use a Web-based collaborative space to build the schedule. Use scheduling software, or spreadsheets and graphics software, to facilitate a more-efficient process. (If you are using scheduling software, you can simply input the predecessors and durations for deadlines, skipping the manual calculations.)

Continued on next page

However, there are benefits in using sticky notes to create a schedule *before* putting it into scheduling software, including:

- It is easier to see the logic of the schedule using sticky notes, especially if there are differing points of view or if the flow has not yet been determined.

- It is easier to see the whole project and for each team member to understand where and how his/her deliverables fit into the project as a whole.

- It is more likely that everyone on the team will understand the flow of the work and their commitments.

- Some people find it difficult to process a lot of numbers so they may be overwhelmed by the large amounts of numbers shown in software schedules; sticky notes are less intimidating.

- Using sticky notes slows the process enough so that each deliverable becomes more tangible.

- Notes and other information can be written directly on the sticky notes to clarify any confusion.

- Changes to the schedule are easier to explore with sticky notes.

- Calculate the "forward pass."

  - Place the deliverables sticky notes on the schedule diagram, one row for each subproject, in sequence. Line up the deliverables horizontally in their subproject rows, and vertically with the milestones at the bottom of the schedule. Begin with the deliverables that have no predecessors. The early start (ES) date for these deliverables will be the project start date.

- Using a calendar and the time required to produce the deliverable, calculate the date each of these deliverables will be completed. Use working days.

- Repeat the process with those deliverables that have predecessors. On the diagram, place these deliverables to begin the next working day after their predecessors are completed. (Note: A deliverable with a one-day duration will begin and end on the *same day*.) Draw arrows to represent the predecessor and successor relationships.

- Continue placing deliverables and calculating the start and end dates until all of the deliverables have been scheduled.

If a deliverable has more than one predecessor, the deliverable can't start until all of the predecessors are complete. Use the early finish (EF) date of the last predecessor to calculate the early start date of the successor.

- Review the major milestones and revise them if necessary. Make sure that imposed deadlines will be met; if they cannot be met, negotiate the schedule with sponsors or other stakeholders.

You chose the milestone dates based on early estimates. Now that you have built a deliverables schedule diagram, you have more detail, and the milestone dates may no longer be valid. Readjust them where possible. If the schedule shows that a critical date can't be met, try to compress the schedule (explained at the end of this chapter) first, then negotiate the cost, scope, or schedule to find the best alternative.

Build the schedule from left to right (i.e., beginning to end). It is not a good idea to work backward from the desired completion date because the project team members may convince themselves that they can meet unrealistic dates in their optimism.

By creating a realistic schedule, you will have credible data to justify resource adjustments when you discuss this with your sponsor.

The Forward Pass

The dates calculated as we've described are the earliest dates each deliverable can begin and the earliest dates each deliverable can finish. This method of scheduling is called a *forward pass*. Unless constrained, the start date of a deliverable is the next working day after the completion date of the latest finish date of all of the predecessors for that deliverable.

Sometimes a particular resource is only available during a certain time, or for other reasons, the beginning and ending dates for a deliverable are chosen rather than calculated. These dates are constrained and should be noted. If additional schedule constraints are imposed, they can affect the critical path and early start, early finish, late start, and late finish dates.

- Calculate the "backward pass."

  - Start with the project completion date you calculated from the forward pass (i.e., the early finish date for the last deliverable in the schedule).

  - For each branch in the diagram, work backward from the completion date of the last deliverable, using the predecessors and durations for each deliverable to calculate the late start (LS) and late finish (LF) dates for each deliverable (i.e., for each deliverable, subtract the duration from the LF to get the LS for that particular deliverable).

2. **Find the critical path.**

   • Compare the ES and EF dates to the LS and LF dates for each deliverable.

   - If the ES/EF dates are the same as the LS/LF dates, the deliverable is located on the critical path and has no float.

   - If the ES/EF dates are not the same as the LS/LF dates, then the number of days between the ES and the LS or between the EF and the LF is the float for that deliverable.

   Beware of rushing the schedule development process—you may not get full understanding and buy-in from your team.

   Do not show artificial early completion dates; doing so will give a false sense of accuracy. Use a realistic start date, predecessors, and durations to calculate the completion date. If this does not meet the required completion date, you can use your realistic schedule to assess your opportunities and negotiate.

Determining Schedule Contingency

Schedule contingency is the amount of time you add to the schedule to reduce the possibility of project delays. You need schedule contingency because even the best and most accurate project estimates are just that—estimates. Determining the amount of contingency is a combination of art and science.

> *They call it an "estimate" for a reason. All estimates are "wrong," although some are better than others. Even if very accurate, an estimate is still an approximation based on assumptions and limited information that is often collected early in the project.*

Why do it?

To allocate time to respond to errors in estimating your project's needs.

The Need for Contingency

Fat, slush, cushion, and *padding* are some of the commonly used terms for contingency. Some of them imply that this added amount of time is a bad thing. Unfortunately, many project managers believe that they need to hide their schedule contingency; otherwise, the project sponsor or customer will remove it.

That's not a good idea. Instead, you should educate your management about the need for contingency and the accuracy of your estimates so that they will understand why you need schedule contingency to be successful. (You might want to adopt the term "contingency reserve" or "reserve" from the PMBOK® Guide.) Otherwise, when the unexpected happens, your project may miss its scheduled end date.

Where Should Contingency Reside?

Many people prefer to build contingency into each deliverable on the schedule. Although this is a common practice, it increases the length of the project because this contingency will almost certainly be used, whether or not the reason for it has occurred. Instead, you should place your project contingency in a common reserve. In that way, the total amount of contingency is generally less than if it were included in every deliverable. To effectively manage the contingency reserve, use a project change management process to allocate the contingency when it is needed.

Comparison Between Common Reserve and Deliverable Contingency

	Contingency in Common Reserve	Contingency in Each Item
Project duration	Shorter	Longer
Project learning	More documentation and data to support lessons learned.	No documentation regarding contingency. Amount of contingency is not defined nor understood.
Use of contingency	Some contingency may be unused.	All contingency is generally used, and often more is needed.
Management control	Project manager develops and controls contingency, with team input.	Individual team members determine and control contingency.
Planning effectiveness	Schedule dates are re-calculated, contingency is adjusted, and risks are monitored during execution.	Completion dates are adjusted when they are missed.

Continued on next page

It is a good practice to have a contingency management process. Some project managers use an internal change management or change control system similar to the one they use to formally change the project management plan.

How do I do it?

1. Review your schedule risk analysis (see Chapter 6) for the amount of potential delay and the probability of occurrence for each significant risk.

2. Ask team members how much contingency, if any, is already included or built into the durations for each deliverable on your schedule.

Project team members generally include some contingency in their estimates, so it's a good idea to ask them whether contingency is part of their durations. On occasion, you may choose to have contingency built into a few deliverables (due to risk), but be careful not to create duplicate contingency time in individual items and in the contingency reserve.

3. Review the critical path and any critical deliverables, using expert judgment to determine the appropriate amount of contingency.

   • If you do not possess the necessary expert judgment yourself, be sure to get help from others who have it, and ask them to review the schedule. Sources of expert judgment include other project managers, subject matter experts, industry standards, sponsors, subproject leaders, vendors or suppliers, and industry or professional organizations.

Although some deliverables may not be on the critical path, they are still essential to the project. Determine their schedule risk, and decide whether more contingency is needed in the schedule.

A simple way to estimate how much contingency you need is by percentage of the total duration. For a low-risk project, 10% may be adequate; for a high-risk project, you may need 25%. (Extremely short or long projects may require a different percentage of contingency for the same risk level and you may need to adjust the amount of contingency. For example, a two-month project may need two weeks' contingency (25%). A six-month project of the same risk level may need only three weeks of contingency, or less than 15%.) You can also use a fixed amount (e.g., a week or a month) or a combination of the two.

To increase commitment, buy-in, and accuracy, be sure to include your project team in the estimating process!

4. **Review the noncritical paths, and determine how much (if any) total contingency you will need to allow for these deliverables.**

   • To determine whether to add contingency, compare the amount of float and the potential delay.

5. **Place the contingency for any specified risks in one common reserve at the end of the schedule.**

6. **Use expert judgment to finalize the amount and location for any additional contingency needed in the schedule.**

©2006 GOAL/QPC

7. **Develop a process and policy for allocating contingency reserve.**

   • Use a project change management process to document and allocate schedule contingency, if you have one. If you don't have one, you will need to develop a process for managing contingency.

8. **Monitor your project risks and performance, and adjust the amount of contingency as needed.**

   • As the project progresses, the amount of risk may vary and you may revise the accuracy of the estimated durations. Reevaluate your schedule contingency periodically during execution or when a major change or unexpected event occurs.

> *Risk responses can be preventive or reactive. Those that prevent risks should already be activities on your schedule. The amount of time for reactive responses—the ones that you plan to activate if a risk occurs—should be factored into your schedule contingency.*
>
> *Decide up front how you will develop and manage schedule contingency. Placing it in a common reserve requires more documentation and discipline, but it usually shortens the overall schedule and eliminates unnecessary use of the reserve.*

How Can You Meet Your Deadline When the Schedule Shows You Can't?

• Compress the schedule to shorten the critical path. (See the section at the end of this chapter on Schedule Compression.)

• Renegotiate the deadline with the sponsor or customer.

Continued on next page

- Examine your assumptions. Maybe there is another way to do the work, or your understanding of the scope or available resources may not be correct.

- Examine and understand the project's constraints. You may be able to negotiate constraints or work around them. Remember, it is OK to ask for clarification! If you know the reason behind a constraint, you may be able to find a workaround solution.

- Negotiate with the sponsor or customer to reduce the scope of the project or to revise the schedule.

- Negotiate with the sponsor, customer, or functional managers to increase resources.

Establishing a Valid Schedule Baseline

Why do it?

To ensure that the final schedule that you measure against is valid.

How do I do it?

1. With your team, perform a review of relevant project documents to prove the schedule start and completion dates are valid.

   - Typical documents to review include the project schedule (to verify dependencies and durations), resource plans (to confirm that resources will support the schedule durations), the project charter and scope statement (to check for missing items), and the risk management plan (to ensure that the contingency reserve is adequate and that risk responses are incorporated in the schedule).

©2006 GOAL/QPC

2. **Discuss concerns and modify the schedule if needed.**
   - Your goal is to feel comfortable that the schedule is workable.

3. **Obtain approval from the project sponsor, project customer(s), and key stakeholders, and create a baseline.**
   - Make sure that revisions to the schedule baseline are only made through formally approved changes.

Managing the Project Schedule During Execution

Why do it?

To stay on top of your project's progress, make wise choices, solve problems, and stay in control of the project, leading it to a successful conclusion.

How do I do it?

1. **Compare the schedule to actual progress to determine whether you need to adjust the schedule or if you need to take action to get back on track.**

2. **Monitor the critical path to uncover potential problems and resolve the problems.**

   Most schedules have some noncritical deliverables with float. You can allow these deliverables to start late without affecting the schedule, thus compensating for deliverables that take longer than planned or helping resolve resource overallocation. Be aware that these deliverables may end up on the critical path if all of the float in that branch is used; changes to these deliverables may affect your project's finish date.

Schedule Compression: Finishing Earlier by Shortening the Critical Path

The following are some of the most effective and logical techniques for shortening the project schedule. Note that if you compress the duration of deliverables without making other adjustments (such as adding resources or decreasing scope), your schedule will be at risk.

- "Crash" the schedule by increasing resources. You can decrease the duration of critical path deliverables and shorten the schedule by assigning overtime work. Or you can assign more than one of the same resource type (such as two designers) as well as multiple, separate resources to a single deliverable. (Note: This practice usually increases the cost of the project.)

- Place deliverables on a "fast track." Plan to work on deliverables concurrently, begin a successor deliverable before the predecessor is completely finished, or change the predecessor relationships. Starting one deliverable before its predecessor is complete may not be ideal, but it can save a lot of time. (Note: This practice usually increases the risk of rework, so discuss this approach with the project sponsor or customer to outline the risks of proceeding without the proper inputs.)

- Decrease the scope of the project. Decreasing the scope can shorten the schedule and cut the duration of some or all of the deliverables on the critical path.

- Break critical path deliverables into more detail or into interim deliverables. Some of these new deliverables may not need to be completed in sequence for the work to progress, and thus you can shorten the critical path.

Chapter 6

Managing
Project Risk

According to the *PMBOK® Guide*, *risk* is "an uncertain event or condition that, if it occurs, has a positive or negative effect on a project's objectives." (Note: An event with a positive impact on project objectives is called an opportunity. Because most people are more concerned with preventing negative impacts, we will only focus on the negative effects of risks.)

It's important to manage project risks, but often we overlook this task or push it aside for other work thought to be more important. Taking the time to identify, analyze, and plan how you will respond to uncertain events can make your projects run smoother and reduce the time you spend managing crises.

A *risk register* is the document that the project manager uses to plan for and manage risk throughout a project. It records information about specific risks for a project, analysis of those risks, and responses to the risks. A typical risk register includes places for:

- The risk name, number, or unique identifier

- The probability of the risk occurring

- The impact on the project if the risk occurs

- A compiled score for the risk

- The identified risk response

- The name of the team member(s) accountable for implementing the risk response

- Any additional comments about the risk or risk response

Risk Register Categories

Risk Number	Risk	Prob- ability	Impact	Score	Responses	Account- able Party	Comments
1	Terry may not	M	L	ML	Accept. Monitor Terry's	Lisa	Not on the critical path.

(Note: A completed risk register is included at the end of this chapter.)

When you need to:	Check the section on:
Define the amount of risk the project can absorb	Establishing risk limits
Define the events that could prevent you from delivering the project according to plan	Identifying project risks
Determine the risks that need your attention	Analyzing project risks
Gain a complete picture of the risks associated with the project	Completing the risk register
Reduce the effects of risks on the project	Developing risk response plans

Establishing Risk Limits

The *Project Management Memory Jogger*™ discusses the risks associated with your ability to create deliverables that conform to the customer's acceptance criteria. In this book we expand that definition to include risks related to not getting the deliverables completed on time and within budget.

Why do it?

To define your project's *risk limits* (i.e., the greatest degree of risk that the schedule and budget can absorb without delivering the project late or over budget).

How do I do it?

1. **Define the parameters for low, medium, and high schedule risks.**

   • For example:

     - Low risk = A late start, late finish, or extended duration on a noncritical path that does not use more than 50% of its float

     - Medium risk = A late start, late finish, or extended duration on a noncritical path that uses more than 50% but less than 100% of its float

     - High risk = Any task on the critical path that starts late, ends late, or takes longer than estimated

2. **Define the parameters for low, medium, and high budget risks.**

   • For example:

     - Low risk = Any cost variance of 0% to 10%

- Medium risk = Any cost variance of 11% to 20%

- High risk = Any cost variance greater than 21%

3. **Define the parameters for technical or scope risks.**

   • For example:

   - Low risk = Some noncritical components may be compromised

   - Medium risk = Functionality is present but may not meet the quality criteria for acceptance

   - High risk = A critical component may not function or may not be present; the product or service is essentially unusable

Some organizations separate scope risks from quality risks. Scope risks refer to the product, and quality risks refer to the performance of the product. Here, we combine these risks under scope.

The parameters listed above are for illustrative purposes only; the values you set for your parameters may vary.

Identifying Project Risks

Why do it?

To identify schedule, cost, and scope risks.

Risk identification occurs throughout a project: during the initiation phase the team identifies high-level risks; during the planning portion of the project the team follows a detailed risk identification process; during project execution the team looks for new risks to any of the project objectives.

How do I do it?

1. **Review the project documentation for indicators of schedule risks.**

   • Schedule risks include risks associated with tasks, paths, or resource availability. Your schedule may be at risk if it contains any of the following:

   - Firm milestones or completion dates that cannot be moved

   - Multiple critical paths

   - Several paths that converge into one point (path convergence)

   - One task that must be completed before several others can start (path divergence)

   - Any overallocated resources

2. **Review the project documentation for indicators of cost risks.**

   • Cost risks include risks associated with cost estimates, cash flow, or resource use. Your budget may be at risk if it contains any of the following:

   - Missing, unrealistic, or inaccurate cost estimates for work described in the WBS

   - Missing or inaccurate documentation of contractual obligations

   - Resource usage over or under budget (for materials, people, etc.)

3. **Review the project documentation for indicators of scope risks.**

   - Scope risks include risks associated with the project's scope, quality, or technical specifications. Your project's scope may be at risk if it contains any of the following:

     - Unvalidated assumptions about quality requirements, technical requirements, or acceptance criteria

     - WBS work not decomposed sufficiently to define the technical requirements and acceptance criteria

     - Unrealistic and unattainable technical requirements using the allocated resources and within the determined timeline

     - Insufficient testing, demonstration, and validation of quality criteria

4. **Using a spreadsheet, document each risk and assign a number or other unique identifier to each risk.**

   - This is the beginning of your risk register.

5. **Review each risk with your team and gather additional information on the risks as needed.**

   - Make sure that team members understand each risk and its implications.

   Make sure that your meetings include team members who tend to be pessimistic. They will see risks that the optimists will miss or ignore.

   Including functional managers, subject matter experts, and others from outside the team can add value to the process by getting a wide range of perspectives.

Analyzing Project Risks

Why do it?

To assess the likelihood that risks will occur and determine the impact to the project if they do.

How do I do it?

1. **With your team, assess the probability that each risk will occur.**

   • Use a high, medium, and low ranking and enter the information into the risk register.

2. **With your team, assess the impact of each risk on the project.**

   • Use a high, medium, and low ranking, following the risk limits that you established in the "Establishing Risk Limits" section of this chapter. Enter this information into the risk register.

3. **Combine the probability and impact assessments to determine a risk score.**

> *If you used the 1–10 ranking described in the* Project Management Memory Jogger™, *translate that into high, medium, and low rankings, using:*
>
> • *Low = 1 to 3*
> • *Medium = 4 to 7*
> • *High = 8 to 10*

Completing the Risk Register

Why do it?

To provide the sponsor and customer, as appropriate, with a complete assessment of the risks associated with the project.

How do I do it?

1. Prioritize your list of risks by putting your high-impact and high-probability risks at the top and the low-impact and low-probability risks at the bottom.

   • This will help you decide which risks to develop risk response plans for. (Risk response plans are described in the next section.)

2. Create a 3x3 chart and plot each risk, by its unique identifier, on the chart.

Sample 3x3 Plot for Risks 1-10

Impact			
High	8	5, 6	2
Medium	4		7
Low	9,10	1	3
	Low	Medium	High

Probability

If you identify many more risks than you expected, that can be good news. You can't respond to risks you don't know about. If you have a lot of risks, it may mean that you did a thorough job of identifying the risks.

Developing Risk Response Plans

Now you can find ways to reduce individual risks and the overall risk to the project. (You will probably not develop detailed risk responses to all risks, especially if you have identified more than 20 risks. Put any low-impact low-probability risks on a "watch list" and revisit them periodically.)

In some instances a response to one risk will take care of several other risks. Other times you will not be so lucky, and you will find that a response to a risk will create a secondary risk that you will need to analyze and respond to.

Why do it?

To reduce the probability or impact (or both) of individual risks and of the overall project risk.

How do I do it?

1. Working with your project team, review your risks to see what actions you can take to reduce or eliminate them.

- Look at four types of actions:
  - *Avoid the risk*: Prevent the situation that causes the risk. Perhaps you can find another approach to the work that will eliminate the risk.
  - *Mitigate the risk*: Look for a way to reduce a risk's probability, impact, or both. If you take action to lower a high-impact medium-probability risk to a low impact and low probability, you are successfully mitigating the risk.
  - *Transfer the risk*: Contractually outsource the work or buy insurance to transfer the risk to a third party.
  - *Accept the risk*: Accept risks that have a low impact or a low probability. You can *passively* accept them by dealing with them only if they occur, or you can *actively* accept them and allot contingency budget or time in the schedule. You may also choose to accept a risk if the cost to avoid, mitigate, or transfer it is too high.

> *Look at your high-impact high-probability risks first, then your high-impact medium-probability risks, and then your high-probability medium-impact risks.*
>
> *If you do not identify a risk, you have accepted it by default. If you choose not to formally respond to a risk, you have accepted it by default.*
>
> *Brainstorming is a great tool to use when you develop risk responses.*

2. **Enter the risk response into the risk register.**

3. Assign accountability to the most appropriate team member.

4. Look to see whether any of the risk responses have initiated any new risks.
   • If they have, enter the new risks in the risk register and put them through the cycle of risk analysis and response development.

Identifying, analyzing, and responding to risks are ongoing activities. They are not something you do once at the beginning of the project and then forget about. As you progress through the project, you will identify new risks and will experience changes to some risks. Other risks will pass, and you can stop worrying about them.

Revisit the entire risk process at predetermined time intervals, when you achieve a significant milestone, when you have a change in scope or change a key team member or stakeholder, or if a major unidentified risk occurs.

Remember, the purpose of risk management is to reduce the likelihood that you will not meet one or more of the project objectives. Usually, high-impact risks are of more concern than high-probability risks.

Sample Risk Register

Risk Number	Risk	Probability*	Impact*	Score*	Response	Accountable Party	Comments
1	Terry may not be available on the dates planned to complete task A. This will cause a one-week delay in the completion.	M	L	ML	Accept. Monitor Terry's availability, but no further action is needed now.	Lisa	Not on the critical path. There are three weeks of float.
2	The cost for the printer is 15% higher than the estimate. This will cause a negative budget variance.	H	M	HM	Mitigate. See if we can negotiate a better rate because of our long-term relationship with the vendor.	Marty	Will need to inform the sponsor if we cannot get the price down, because a 15% overage is significant.
3	If the prototype does not function as planned we will have to re-work it, causing a six-week delay.	L	H	LH	Mitigate. Put in an interim plan review, and check the functionality at each phase.	Lucia	This is a critical path item. If it is late, the project completion date is impacted.

*This risk register uses the definitions of high, medium, and low given earlier.

©2006 GOAL/QPC

Chapter 7

Controlling
Project Progress

When pilots file a flight plan, they intend to stay close to it—but not exactly on it. In fact, about 90% of the time, the plane is not directly on course with the flight plan, but it is within an acceptable range. If pilots fly out of the acceptable range, they take corrective action or file a new flight plan as appropriate.

It is the same way with projects. The project baselines are guides for the project manager. Not every activity will start on the exact date it was scheduled, and rarely are budgets allocated down to the penny. But it is important for the project manager to stay as close to the plan as possible. If the plan is significantly off track, the project manager and project team will take corrective action to get back on track. If the plan is too far off track, the project manager and team will need to replan the work.

When you need to:	Check the section on:
Establish a baseline to measure integrated project performance	Creating a performance measurement baseline
Establish whether project performance is acceptable	Reviewing performance variances
Assess the degree of project variance	Reviewing performance indices

Continued on next page

When you need to:	Check the section on:
Estimate future performance	Developing a forecast
Bring the plan back to acceptable performance levels	Taking preventive and corrective actions
Create new project expectations	Establishing new baselines for the project

Creating a Performance Measurement Baseline

Why do it?

To establish an integrated baseline to measure schedule progress and cost performance. Before you can assess your progress, you need a baseline to compare your progress to. Your integrated baseline should integrate information on your project scope, schedule, and costs. Measuring against this baseline is how you will know whether your project is performing as planned or whether you need to take corrective action.

How do I do it?

1. **Create a chart of WBS work packages.**

   • Make sure that each work package has:

   - An estimated cost

   - An accountable person

   - A way to measure completion

Sample WBS Work Package

> ### *Deliverable E*
> Estimated Cost: $400
>
> Accountable Person: Brian S.
>
> Completion Measurement:
> 3 interim deliverables
> (25%, 50%, 25%)

Work with team members to determine the cost estimate for each deliverable. You may need additional resources (i.e., vendors, external expertise, quotes from outside the organization, and information from past projects) to assist in developing your estimates.

- Meet with the accountable person for each deliverable to establish how you will measure its progress and define the acceptance criteria. The following are the three most common ways of measuring progress:
  - Measure the deliverable's percent complete. (The percent complete is an estimate of the amount of work already completed, expressed as a percentage.)
  - Set up interim weighted subdeliverables, and have each one represent an agreed-upon percent complete. For example, you may have three interim deliverables, two weighted at 25% of the value and one weighted at 50% of the value.
  - Use a fixed formula (e.g., 25% credit for starting an activity and 75% for finishing it, or 0/100% to show that no credit is earned until the activity is complete).

Be sure to define the level of detail you will use for measuring progress; you can measure at the activity level, the work package level, or even the project level.

When you ask your team members how far along they are and they give you a percent complete without any objective evidence, it would be wise to check the results yourself. Otherwise, you may be unpleasantly surprised, as the deliverable nears completion, to find that they estimate they are 90% complete and you estimate they are only 60% complete. (If you set objective criteria while creating your baseline, this should not be a problem. Having objective criteria, agreed upon by the project manager and the team members, helps to ensure measurable progress.)

Sample Chart of WBS Work Packages

Deliverable	Duration (weeks)	Predecessor	Planned* Value	Earned Value* Measurement Method
A	3	—	$600	Schedule percent complete- 33% each week
B	4	A	$400	Physical percent complete, even distribution
C	2	B	$300	Physical percent complete, even distribution
D	1	B	$200	0/100%
E	3	D	$400	3 weighted interim deliverables: 1st = 25%, 2nd = 50%, 3rd = 25%

*Planned value and earned value are explained later in this section.

2. **Create a *performance measurement baseline.***

   - Create a chart that shows each deliverable across a time line, along with the cost of the deliverable. This will show you the *planned value* (PV) spread across time.

   - At the bottom of the chart, tabulate the planned value to be accomplished per reporting cycle, along with the cumulative value. (Your cumulative value should equal the project budget.)

   - Plot the data from the chart as a line graph, with the value (in dollars) as the y-axis and the duration (in the time periods you used as column headers in your chart) as the x-axis.

3. **Establish control limits.**

   - Define the boundaries that will serve as indicators for when your schedule or cost is too far from the baseline. (It is unlikely you will be exactly on schedule or exactly on budget throughout your project.)

   > *Whether you use the risk limits discussed in Chapter 6 or create your own definitions, you should establish some measurement criteria to indicate when your project performance is heading out of control.*

4. **Measure your project progress at any point in the project by comparing the planned value (from the line graph) with the earned value (defined on next page).**

Your performance measurement baseline is not a schedule, nor is it a budget. Instead, it shows you how to measure integrated performance on your project.

Planned Value and Earned Value

The planned value (PV) is the dollar value you *expect* (plan) to earn at a given point in time. Earned value (EV) is the dollar value you *actually earn* at a given point in time.

For example, if you plan to paint 40 houses in a subdivision and are to be paid $80,000 for the job, you can equate each house you paint as worth $2000. Your schedule shows that you expect to complete 10 houses per week. This equals $20,000 of planned value per week. If, at the end of the second week, you only have 18 houses painted (instead of the expected 20 houses), your earned value is only $36,000, even though your planned value was $40,000.

Earned value is also different from what you have spent. For example, let's say you have a deliverable that was supposed to take two weeks and cost $300. At the end of the first week you have accomplished 33% of the work. No matter what you have spent, you have earned $100 worth of value.

Chart of Deliverables
for the Performance Measurement Baseline

Deliverable	1	2	3	4	5	6	7	8	9	10	11
A	$200	$200	$200								
B				$100	$100	$100	$100				
C								$150	$150		
D								$200			
E									$100	$200	$100
PV per week	$200	$200	$200	$100	$100	$100	$100	$350	$250	$200	$100
Cumulative PV	$200	$400	$600	$700	$800	$900	$1000	$1350	$1600	$1800	$1900

Notes:

- Deliverable A has three weeks' duration, with 33% of the value planned each week. The PV for the deliverable is $600; therefore, each week should produce $200 worth of value.
- Deliverable B has four weeks' duration and has a planned value of $400. We assume an even distribution of value, $100 per week.
- Deliverable C follows the same logic as deliverable B.
- Deliverable D is only one week in duration, so we plan to achieve all of the value in that week.
- Deliverable E has three interim deliverables. The total deliverable value is $400, and the interim deliverables are weighted to show the percentage of value attained with each milestone. Suppose deliverable E is to create a training manual. The first interim deliverable is the detailed outline, which has a PV of $100. The second interim deliverable is the first draft, which has a value of $200, and the final interim deliverable is the finished manuscript, with a value of $100, for a total cumulative planned value of $400.

A Performance Measurement Baseline for the Chart of Deliverables on the Previous Page

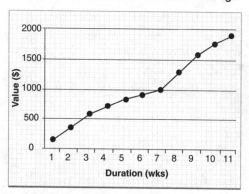

Reviewing Performance Variances

Why do it?

To measure your planned schedule performance against your actual schedule performance and calculate what it actually cost to achieve that performance. (This comparison will indicate whether you are ahead or behind schedule, and over or under budget.)

How do I do it?

1. **During planning, establish what information to collect and how often you need to collect it from the progress reports and status reports of your team.**

   • Consider collecting information on:
     - Deliverables that have started or finished during the reporting period

- The status of deliverables in progress
- The costs incurred during the reporting period

Focus on collecting meaningful information about your project status, not just data that is easy to collect. In addition to the information listed above, you should collect information on risks and issues, including:

- *New risks and issues that have arisen.*

- *A change in the status of a risk or issue.*

- *Risks or issues that are closed.*

Be sure that you add this information to your risk register.

2. **Use the planned value from the performance measurement baseline to calculate the value of what you** *expect* **to have earned during the reporting period.**

Remember – this may be different from what you have spent.

3. **Determine your earned value for each deliverable by using the earned value measurement method you've established in the previous section.**

4. **Assess your schedule variance by subtracting your planned value (derived from your performance measurement baseline) from your earned value (derived from your performance reports).**

Schedule Variance = Earned Value – Planned Value,
or SV = EV – PV

5. **Assess your budget variance by subtracting your actual costs (derived from your cost accounting system) from your earned value.**

Cost Variance = Earned Value – Actual Cost,
or CV = EV – AC

When you review variances, a negative variance always indicates bad news; a positive variance might indicate good news, but not necessarily. (You may have a favorable cost variance, but perhaps it is because you did not receive a piece of equipment you had planned to receive, and therefore have not incurred the cost for it.)

Sample Review of Performance Variances

Here's a performance variance review process that uses the sample performance measurement baseline we created previously. If we are reviewing the performance variance for deliverables A and B at the end of week 5, we will see that:

Deliverable	Duration	Predecessor	Planned Value	Earned Value Measurement Method
A	3	—	$600	33% of each week
B	4	A	$400	Percent complete, even distribution

Deliverable	1	2	3	4	5
A	$200	$200	$200		
B				$100	$100

Our status reports show that we have finished deliverable A and that deliverable B is 40% complete. Our accounting records show that we have spent $580 completing deliverable A, and $210 so far on deliverable B. Using our variance equations, we find:

Deliverable A
PV = $600
EV = $600 (because deliverable A is complete)
AC = $580
SV for deliverable A = $600 – $600 = $0
CV for deliverable A = $600 – $580 = $20

Deliverable B
PV = $200
EV = $160 (because deliverable B is only 40% complete, the EV is
    40% of the planned value of $400 = $160)
AC = $210
SV for deliverable B = $160 – $200 = –$40
CV for deliverable B = $160 – $210 = –$50

Continued on next page

©2006 GOAL/QPC

This information tells us:

- Deliverable A is complete. When a deliverable is complete, no matter when it is finished, it has always earned what was planned, so the schedule variance is $0.
- Deliverable A finished under budget (since the cost variance is a positive number).
- Deliverable B is behind schedule and over budget (since both the schedule variance and cost variance are negative numbers). At the end of week 5, we planned to have $200 worth of work accomplished, and we accomplished only $160 worth of work. We spent $210 to earn $160 worth of work.
- If deliverable B is on the critical path and we do not correct the schedule problem, the project will be late.

Note that the information does not tell us whether deliverable A finished on time; it tells us only that, at this point, it is complete. The information also tells us that we have a problem with deliverable B, but it does not tell us what it is, why we have it, or how to solve it. We would have to investigate further.

You should always find the root cause of any variances that are outside of the control limits, and work to correct it as soon as possible. When investigating root cause(s), look at all possibilities, including poor estimates, poor performance, and unrecognized changes in scope, schedule, or cost.

For a quick visual display of your project performance, you can chart your earned value progress next to your planned value progress on your performance measurement baseline. You can also chart what you have actually spent on the same chart. This will show you at a glance whether you are ahead or behind schedule, or over or under cost.

Reviewing Performance Indices

Project Sponsor · Project Manager · Team Member

Why do it?

To gain a common perspective on project performance and to compare performance across projects, deliverables, and various levels of the WBS.

> An index normalizes schedule and cost performance indicators. You can use an index (or indices) to compare the performance of multiple projects in an organization. A variance of $1000 may not be a problem on a project with a $1,000,000 budget, but it could be a problem on a project with a $10,000 budget.

How do I do it?

1. Assess your schedule performance index by dividing your earned value by your planned value.

   Schedule Performance Index = $\dfrac{\text{Earned Value}}{\text{Planned Value}}$

   or SPI = $\dfrac{EV}{PV}$

2. Assess your cost performance index by dividing your earned value by your actual costs.

   Cost Performance Index = $\dfrac{\text{Earned Value}}{\text{Actual Cost}}$

   or CPI = $\dfrac{EV}{AC}$

> When you review indices, an index less than 1.0 indicates bad news. An index greater than 1.0 does not necessarily indicate good news, although it might.

©2006 GOAL/QPC

An index other than 1.0 indicates that performance is not proceeding according to plan but it does not tell you what the problem is. In fact, what seems to be a performance issue might be an estimating issue. (Perhaps the original duration estimates were too aggressive, or maybe you've experienced scope creep without allocating extra time or budget.)

Sample Review of Performance Indices

Using the information from the variance equations, we come up with the following performance indices for our example:

Deliverable A
Schedule performance index (SPI) = EV/PV = $600/$600 = 1.0
Cost performance index (CPI) = EV/AC = $600/$580 = 1.03

Deliverable B
Schedule performance index (SPI) = $160/$200 = 0.8
Cost performance index (CPI) = $160/$210 = 0.76

This information tells us:

• Deliverable A is complete. When a deliverable is complete, no matter when it is finished, it has always earned what was planned, so the schedule performance index will be 1.0. (You do not get credit for finishing early, nor do you carry bad performance forward after a deliverable is complete.)

• Deliverable A budget performance will remain positive throughout the rest of the project (since the task is complete).

• Deliverable B is running 20% behind schedule. (An SPI of 0.8 tells us that we were only 80% efficient.)

• For every dollar spent on deliverable B, the team is realizing only $0.76 worth of value.

While these earned value measurements do not reflect the quality of the deliverables, the acceptance criteria defined for each deliverable address the deliverables' quality.

Developing a Forecast

Project Sponsor **Project Manager** **Team Member**

Why do it?

To help in making decisions that can impact the final duration and cost while there is still time to develop options.

How do I do it?

1. **Develop an** *estimate at completion* **(EAC) to estimate the final cost of the project.**

   - If you think that future project cost performance will continue in the same manner as past performance, divide the total *budget at completion* (BAC) by the cost performance index (i.e., EAC = BAC/CPI). (Note: The BAC is the end point of your planned value. In our example, it is $1900.)

   - If you think the spending variance will not recur, then subtract what you have earned (EV) from the BAC and then add what you have already spent (i.e., EAC = (BAC – EV) +AC).

   - If you believe the original cost estimates to be inaccurate, then add what you have spent (AC) and develop new *estimates to complete* (ETC) (i.e., EAC = ETC + AC).

2. **Develop an** *estimated duration at completion* **(EDAC) to estimate when the project will be completed.**

   - If the future schedule performance will continue in the same manner as past performance, divide the total *estimated duration* (ED) of the project by the SPI (i.e., EDAC = ED/SPI).

   - If the duration variance is only on one or a few activities, then subtract the variance on the critical path from the total estimated duration (i.e., EDAC = ED – SV).

- If you believe the original duration estimates to be inaccurate, then add the current duration to a new estimated duration.

> *For EDAC, use only the information on the critical path.*

> *EDAC has not been proven to be as reliable as the EAC calculation. It is not used as much as EAC and may not be appropriate for all projects. It's tricky to forecast duration variance because you can do activities in parallel that were scheduled sequentially (fast tracking), or you can work overtime, add more resources, and/or bring in outside help (crashing), to shorten the remaining schedule.*

Sample Forecast

Using the information discussed previously, we can come up with the following forecast numbers:

1. If the future cost performance is expected to continue like past performance, then EAC = BAC/CPI so 1900/0.96 = $1979. (We derived the project CPI by adding the AC for both deliverables and dividing it by the EV for both deliverables.)

2. If future cost performance is not expected to resemble past performance, then EAC = (BAC – EV) + AC so (1900 – 760) + 810 = $1950.

3. If future schedule performance is expected to resemble past performance, than EDAC = ED/SPI so 11/0.95 = 11.57 weeks. (We derived the project SPI by adding the PV for both deliverables and dividing it by the EV for both deliverables.)

4. If future schedule performance is not expected to resemble past performance, then EDAC = ED – SV so 11 – (–1) = 12 weeks. (We took the SPI for deliverable B, which is on the critical path, and divided the duration of deliverable B (4 weeks) by the SPI (0.8) to come up with a new duration of 5 weeks. We subtracted the 1-week difference between the planned duration and the estimated duration for deliverable B from the project as a whole.)

Earned value management assumes that the original estimates were correct and that negative variances are due to performance problems, but this is not always the case. Unfavorable variances and indices could mean that the original budget was inaccurate, the baseline schedule was overly optimistic, a risk event caused a schedule delay, or the scope increased but the performance measurement baseline was not updated to reflect the change. You must always understand the reasons for variances; only with this understanding can you take effective measures to improve performance.

You may need to develop a new forecast if you have:

- Variances that are significant

- A change in scope

- A risk that occurs, causing a significant cost or schedule delay

Taking Preventive and Corrective Actions

Why do it?

To prevent schedule, cost, or quality variances, or to get the project back on track.

Correcting Negative Schedule Variances

How do I do it?

1. Verify that there are enough qualified people available to complete the work.

2. Add resources to deliverables that are on the critical path to expedite completion.

3. Do activities in parallel, or overlap activities that were scheduled sequentially.

4. Break tasks into smaller pieces, and revise the schedule to perform activities concurrently.

5. Monitor the schedule more often.

Correcting Negative Costs Variances

How do I do it?

1. To improve accuracy, increase the detail in the cost estimate.

2. Examine future expenditures to look for a way to reduce costs.

3. Investigate the root cause of the cost overage, and find a way to mitigate it.

4. Seek ways to do the remaining work more efficiently.

Correcting Deliverables That Do Not Meet Acceptance Criteria

How do I do it?

1. Increase the number of technical or customer reviews or approvals.

2. Increase the amount of detail in descriptions of the deliverables.

3. Revisit the acceptance criteria to determine if they are appropriate.

4. Revisit the measurement methods to determine if they are appropriate.

Establishing New Baselines for the Project

Why do it?

To develop new estimates for the schedule and budget in response to a scope change or if the original estimates are so inaccurate that measuring performance against them does not provide valid or reliable information.

 Be sure to include team members when you establish new baselines.

If the Scope Has Changed

How do I do it?

1. Gather complete and accurate requirements for any new deliverables.

2. Develop acceptance criteria.

3. Update the WBS.

4. Update the resource requirements.

5. Develop schedule estimates for the new scope components and any necessary rework.

6. Develop cost estimates for the new components or rework.

7. Review the new deliverables, schedule, and cost estimates for risks.
   - Analyze the risks.
   - Develop responses to the risks.

8. Develop a new performance measurement baseline based on the new information.

> It is important to maintain the original baseline for historical purposes. It will be an input to your lessons-learned document at the end of the project.

If the Scope Has Not Changed

How do I do it?

1. Determine the root cause of the failure to meet your original estimates.

2. Use your experience from this project to develop new, more realistic estimates to use as a baseline for the duration of the project.

> You may need to establish a new baseline if any of the following things happen:
>
> - You need to clarify requirements.
>
> - The original estimates are inaccurate.

Continued on next page

- *You lack the resources that were originally called for.*

- *You haven't planned well.*

- *A risk event occurs.*

Only compare work going forward to the new baseline; do not compare work that is already completed.

Chapter 8

Improving
Team Communication

Communication is the process people use to share information and feelings via verbal, written, and nonverbal cues. It is more productive to view communication as an *outcome* rather than as an event. This view puts the responsibility on the speaker to send the clearest message possible.

We've found it helpful to look at communication as a three-part process: delivering information, receiving information, and exchanging feedback.

When you need to:	Check the section on:
Construct your message in clear language and identify and remove barriers that listeners may have	Delivering information effectively
Understand the meaning of another person's words and the ideas and feelings behind them	Effective listening
Improve communication when the speaker has strong feelings, is agitated, or needs to talk about a situation	Active listening
Encourage someone to change an undesirable behavior or repeat a desired behavior	Giving constructive feedback
Encourage constructive feedback of your own behavior	Receiving feedback

Delivering Information Effectively

Project Manager | Team Member | Project Sponsor | Senior Mgmt

Why do it?

To reduce misunderstandings by customers, stakeholders, and project team members, and help prevent rework. It's critical to be as precise as possible, especially when you document the scope and acceptance criteria for deliverables.

> It is important to use these information delivery techniques whenever time permits. Remember, a message that is not delivered properly can cause many time-consuming problems at a later point in time.

How do I do it?

1. **When communicating with project team members in person or in writing, use objective language.**

   • Apply the "SMART" test to check whether your language is objective. Ask if your language is:

     - **S**pecific,

     - **M**easurable,

     - **A**chievable,

     - **R**ealistic, and

     - **T**angible.

Objective Language vs. Subjective Language

Highly successful project managers use objective, clear, simple, and specific language to clarify and improve the quality of the information they deliver. Objective information is precise and uses numbers or very specific indicators, minimizing the chance of misinterpretation. Examples of objective terms are "30 seconds or less," "at least 95 out of 100," "yes," and "no."

In contrast, subjective information uses vaguely defined terms, such as "big," "fast," "good," and "accurate." Such terms are open to interpretation and can lead to false agreement.

2. **Identify and remove *listening filters* that may block listeners from hearing your intended message.**

   • A listening filter can discount, change, or even eliminate information, preventing effective communication. Listening filters include the listeners':

     - Belief systems

     - Assumptions

     - Culture

     - Education

     - Familiarity with the topic and speaker

     - Emotional state

     - Trust in the speaker

3. **Deliver the information nonverbally as well as verbally.**

   • Be conscious of unspoken messages that you may be sending.

Nonverbal Communication

According to research done by Albert Mehrabian of UCLA, words make up only 7% of the content of a message. Your facial expression and body language deliver 55% of your message, and your tone of voice makes up 38%. This means that you must pay close attention to these nonverbal cues. Be aware of your posture, your proximity to listeners, your facial expression, and the volume, tempo, and tone of your voice. Also take advantage of visual aids if possible.

Effective Listening

We often take good listening skills for granted. We assume that everyone can listen adequately, but it requires training to become careful listeners and adapt our listening style to a specific situation. Most people receive more training and education in reading and speaking than in listening.

Effective listening means paying close attention to verbal and nonverbal cues, to understand the other person's position and convey your understanding of the communication. With practice, you can improve and strengthen this skill.

Why do it?

To improve communication by understanding the meaning of another person's words and the ideas and feelings behind them.

©2006 GOAL/QPC

How do I do it?

1. Focus on the speaker and what he or she is saying.

2. Use attentive behaviors, such as eye contact and an open posture.

3. Ask open or clarifying questions to make sure that you understand the speaker's meaning.

4. Do not multitask or accept interruptions during the conversation.

Open-Ended Questions vs. Limiting Questions

Open-ended questions—such as "What issues are affecting your schedule?"—ask for discussion. Open-ended questions are helpful when you want to:

*   Encourage others to talk more
*   Learn more about a topic
*   Engage the other person in a conversation

Open-ended questions are also useful when you're solving problems, defining requirements, influencing others' opinions, learning new information, and selling.

In contrast, closed-ended or limiting questions ask for short answers (often yes or no). Examples include "Is your project on schedule?" or "Would you like some assistance with your schedule?" Limiting questions are helpful when you want to:

*   End or control the conversation
*   Receive a yes or no answer
*   Focus the other person on an action or a decision

Limiting questions are also useful when you're negotiating or trying to influence someone.

Active Listening

Active listening is a variation of effective listening that focuses on the emotions of the speaker. Active listening uses paraphrasing, and the listener does not ask questions or offer information or advice.

Why do it?

To improve communication when the speaker has strong feelings, is agitated, or needs to talk about a situation to process it out loud. Active listening is useful when emotions are high and logic or reasoning may not be effective. Active listening defuses emotions by allowing the speaker to calm down and begin problem solving.

> *Effective listening is best used in normal, everyday conversation, while using active listening in normal conversation is awkward, annoying, and unproductive.*

How do I do it?

1. In a conversation with someone who is emotionally charged, repeat the speaker's message in your own words, but don't add content. Allow the speaker to focus on his or her own thoughts.

2. Allow the person to freely express emotions and manage his or her own feelings.

> *You don't have to "rescue" the speaker or take ownership of the problem.*

©2006 GOAL/QPC

3. **Ask permission before giving advice, and don't rush the conversation.**

   - Do not share your own story or experiences unless asked directly.

4. **Avoid communication roadblocks.**

   - Communication roadblocks are statements that trigger defensiveness or end the conversation. Examples include ordering, commanding, warning, threatening, moralizing, lecturing, persuading, blaming, and criticizing. In emotionally charged situations, logical arguments—even advising or giving solutions—can also be roadblocks. Think about how you would feel if someone interrupted you with one of these roadblocks when you were trying to get your thoughts straight or sort out a problem.

Giving Constructive Feedback

When you give *constructive feedback*, you describe the other person's behavior, express your feelings about it, and explain how it affects you, without judging or placing blame. You explain the effect of the behavior and help the other person find a solution to the problem. Your goal is to maintain respect for both parties and avoid taking ownership of the problem; constructive feedback keeps ownership of the problem with the person whose behavior you want to change.

Constructive feedback has a number of benefits. It preserves the relationship and sets the stage for the other person to come up with alternatives. It helps both parties understand the other's point of view, and it defuses emotions. If the message is accurately and carefully composed, the constructive feedback is objective and cannot be disputed.

Constructive feedback is also suitable to recognize someone for doing a good job. It is much more effective than empty praise because it is specific, tangible, easier to understand, and more believable than generic or general compliments.

Why do it?

To effectively encourage someone to change an undesirable behavior or repeat a desired behavior.

How do I do it?

1. **Prepare for the discussion and construct the message.**

   • Identify your motives and intentions. Be very clear with yourself about what you want to happen as a result of the discussion. Ask yourself, "What are my motives for providing this feedback? What do I hope to accomplish?"

Planning is critical for a successful outcome. You may also have emotions about the issue, so make sure you are prepared.

   • Construct the message.

   - Provide the person with an objective example of the behavior, described in objective language. Use phrasing such as "When you. . .," that includes an objective description of the behavior.

An objective description of behavior will describe what a video would see, with no judgment, evaluation, or opinion.

- Describe the feelings you have when the other person exhibits the problem behavior. Use the phrase "...I feel..." to describe the way you feel as a result of the behavior.

- Describe the tangible effects or consequences of the behavior on you or the team. Include the phrase "...because..." that explains these tangible effects.

A Sample Constructive Feedback Message

> When you *come late to our project team meeting*, I feel *frustrated* because *you may miss something important and we will need to repeat information for you, causing the meeting to take longer.*

When appropriate, you can start with the "I feel..." part of the message to emphasize the behavior's emotional impact on you. (This approach is most often used in personal or family relationships.)

- Rehearse the message with someone before delivering it, and ask for feedback. (The most difficult part of constructing the message is to find a nonjudgmental description of the other person's behavior.)

Be sure to practice or rehearse with someone, even if it's the family cat.

2. **Choose an appropriate time and location, in a reasonably private setting, to deliver the message.**

   • Deliver the message without apologies or heightened emotion. It is OK to use notes.

   • If the person reacts defensively or offensively, practice active listening to understand his or her perspective. Active listening also helps to calm the other person down, allowing you to regroup and redeliver the message.

 Be sure to stay on topic. Don't be distracted by other issues.

3. **Resolve the problem.**

   • Discuss options for acceptable behavior, asking for suggestions from the other person. Agree on the next steps you should both take.

   • Repeat the message, active listening, and discussion steps if necessary until your message has been delivered, understood, and has led to a resolution.

   • End the discussion with one of the following:

     - An agreement to meet and discuss the matter further at another time

     - An agreement to disagree without hard feelings

     - A move to more-formal conflict resolution procedures that will be discussed later

     - A solution to the problem

> *If you make any agreements, document them and send a copy to the other person, to ensure clear, mutual understanding.*

 If there are no tangible effects, it means that you have a conflict of values. A values conflict in a business situation or on a project usually ends in an agreement to disagree. To preserve the relationship, use active listening if there are strong feelings about the difference of opinion.

Receiving Feedback

Communicating effectively includes helping others deliver feedback constructively to you. The person giving feedback may not have the skills for developing and delivering a constructive feedback message. As a person who has these skills, you need to use both effective listening and active listening to achieve a professional and successful outcome.

Why do it?

To improve communication by encouraging constructive feedback of your own behavior.

How do I do it?

1. Acknowledge the facts.

2. Stay calm and focus on listening.

   • Don't argue or be defensive.

3. Offer opinions only when asked.

4. **Take time to absorb the message before you react.**

   • If you are asked a question, ask whether it is OK to answer it later to allow you to process your thoughts without interrupting the conversation.

5. **Be sure you understand the message before evaluating it.**

6. **Be attentive to the other person's point of view.**

7. **Say "thank you."**

You can always respond later to feedback. Ask for time to consider it and to prepare a response, if needed.

Chapter 9

Conducting Negotiations
and Resolving Conflict

Negotiation is a rational process that you use to resolve intellectual differences or conflicts of opinion or beliefs. It is central to any effort involving a number of people. A successful project manager must be a skilled negotiator to ensure that all team members are working toward the same goal.

When you need to:	Check the section on:
Find a mutually acceptable resolution to conflicts or differences	Negotiating for mutual benefit
Keep projects on track by finding mutually acceptable solutions to conflicts between team members and/or stakeholders	Resolving conflict

Negotiating for Mutual Benefit

Why do it?

To solve problems, avoid litigation, and find a mutually acceptable resolution to conflicts or differences.

If you are inflexible when negotiating, you may damage a relationship, but if you are not firm and clear enough about your needs, you may give too many concessions to the other party (which could result in resentment or unworkable agreements or contracts). Work to develop well-executed negotiations that preserve relationships and lead to mutually beneficial agreements.

How do I do it?

1. **Identify the constraints, limits, and boundaries of the negotiation.**

   • Include legal or regulatory requirements, procedural limitations, financial barriers, and budget limits.

2. **Take care of preparation and logistics.**

   • Research possible outcomes and estimate their impact and consequences.

   • Be well prepared with facts and information.

   • Determine the minimum and maximum you will take or you can give.

   • Know what you are authorized to offer.

   • If possible, meet at a neutral location.

   • Allow enough time to fully explore the situation and options.

   • Know your and the other party's worst-case option if negotiation fails.

Obtain approval in advance from others when negotiating on their behalf.

©2006 GOAL/QPC

3. **Eliminate obstacles to a rational exchange.**

   • Separate the personalities, including your own, from the problem.

   • Understand your assumptions and belief systems.

   • Establish the best person-to-person relationship possible, and assume positive intentions from the other side.

   • Don't be partial to any one solution or position.

   • Try to see the situation from the other person's point of view.

   • Don't try to take advantage of the other person.

   • Be prepared to question your opinions and beliefs.

   • Be open-minded.

4. **Keep the focus on interests and underlying needs.**

   • Base the negotiations on the interests of the parties involved, not their feelings about the situation.

   • Avoid arguing over positions. Use objective criteria, standards, and logic.

   • Be sure to clarify interests, needs, hopes, and desires.

5. **Offer reasonable options and solutions.**

   • Make sure that your reasonable solutions meet all underlying needs. Incorporate any new information obtained during the negotiation into your discussion.

6. **When you have completed the negotiation, document the results and agreements, and distribute copies to the appropriate people. Continue to monitor results and evaluate how the results are working.**

Nonthreatening Language

Negotiation often involves resistance and emotion. It's good to have a repertoire of nonthreatening language to help defuse tension and focus attention on the merits of the issue. Here are some examples:

"Please correct me if I am wrong."

"We appreciate what you have done for us."

"Could I ask a few questions to see if my facts are right?"

"Let me see if I understand what you're saying."

"Let me show you where I am having trouble following your reasoning."

"Let me get back to you."

"Here is what I am thinking."

"Will that work for you?"

"What is your reaction to what I am saying?"

"How does that sound to you?"

"It has been a pleasure dealing with you."

When you're negotiating, keep the following principles in mind:

- *Ask questions, and listen carefully to the answers.*
- *Make it your goal to arrive at a solution that benefits both parties.*
- *Remember that negotiation is not warfare; it is part of an ongoing relationship.*
- *Be observant and analyze what is going on.*
- *Be flexible.*
- *Make sure you know what you want and don't want.*
- *If you become upset, take time out to think through your position.*

©2006 GOAL/QPC

Resolving Conflict

Project managers often find themselves in situations where there is a conflict between team members (i.e., an incompatibility of opinions or principles). To manage the project efficiently, you must negotiate to resolve this kind of serious disagreement or argument.

Why do it?

To keep projects on track by finding mutually acceptable solutions to conflicts between team members and/or stakeholders.

How do I do it?

1. **Identify and define the conflict.**

   • Share feelings and facts, and explain positions and reasons.

   • Agree on and accept the definition of the problem.

 To enhance communication, use the effective listening techniques you learned in Chapter 8.

2. **Develop alternative solutions.**

   • Brainstorm ideas, but withhold evaluation and judgment about what might work.

3. **Evaluate the possible solutions.**

   • Be honest, and test your ideas.

> *To help you evaluate your ideas, use decision-making tools such as the prioritization matrices found in* The Memory Jogger™ II: A Pocket Guide of Tools for Continuous Improvement and Effective Planning *by GOAL/QPC.*

4. **Choose a solution without persuading or pushing for your favorite.**
   • Verify that you have a mutual understanding of the solution, and make a mutual commitment.

> *Be sure to also verify your assumptions about the solution.*

5. **Implement the solution.**
   • Develop an action plan (who, what, and when), and commit to carry it out.

6. **Follow up and evaluate the situation, reviewing facts and feelings.**
   • If you want to modify the initial decision, obtain mutual agreement before doing so.

7. **If the solution is not adequate, repeat steps 1–6.**

Understanding Conflict Modes

According to Kenneth Wayne Thomas and Ralph Kilmann, authors of the *Thomas-Kilmann Conflict Mode Instrument* (CPP, Inc. and Davies-Black Publishing, Mountain View, CA), there are five basic ways of responding to conflict. Effective project managers understand that responding to conflict is a choice, and they choose the appropriate mode according to the project's objectives and circumstances.

Continued on next page

Conflict Modes and Outcomes

Conflict Handling Mode	Effect on Self/Other	Use When:	Benefits	Disadvantages
Avoidance (Avoid the conflict)	Lose/Lose	You need a cooling-off period, you can't win, or you don't care	Reduces stress	Others may resent being ignored; the issue is never resolved
Accommodation (Let the other side win)	Lose/Win	The relationship is more important than the issue, or you can't win	Restores harmony	Others may exploit you
Compromise (Have both parties give up something)	Win Some/Lose Some	You are on equal footing and you want to maintain a relationship	Equal gains and losses for both sides	The issue is not resolved
Competition (Have your needs met at the expense of others)	Win/Lose	You have power, the need is urgent, or you are not concerned about the relationship	Meets your needs	Others are probably resentful
Collaboration (Have the needs of both sides met)	Win/Win	You have time to find a win/win situation	Best win/win synergy	Takes more time

Effective project managers choose the best strategic response to conflicts and are prepared when conflicts arise. Your response to conflict should be a thoughtful, deliberate choice. When your choice for handling conflict is compromise or collaboration, you need to engage the other person in a conflict resolution process. Competition (trying to win), avoidance (doing nothing or ignoring the conflict), and accommodation (giving in to the others side) do not require a process.

If you're preparing for compromise or collaboration, be sure to ask yourself:

- *Do you believe that the other person has a valid, reasonable, rational position?*

- *Are you willing to find a win/win solution to the problem?*

- *Do you believe that there is a possible solution that satisfies both parties?*

- *Are you willing to explore solutions other than the one you already have?*

- *Do you know and understand your own motives and belief systems?*

- *Do both parties have a feeling of safety?*

- *Do you understand both the facts (objective data) and the opinions (subjective data)?*

Chapter 10

Applying Effective
Leadership to Projects

The project manager and sponsor share the responsibility for the success of the project with the subproject leaders, the project team, functional and resource managers, suppliers, and stakeholders. It is imperative that all of the people involved in the project exhibit the characteristics of leaders and demonstrate and practice leadership behaviors. As a project professional, you will depend on others to define, plan, execute, report on, and complete their parts of the project's work. Often, you don't have the authority to get others to put in the extra effort it takes to meet your project objectives, so you need to motivate them to gain their willing and voluntary cooperation. Motivating team members is easier if you have a basic understanding of how to wield influence and power, create rapport, adapt your leadership style, and help people react to change.

When you need to:	Check the section on:
Improve project efficiency and results by building strong interpersonal relationships with team members	Enhancing your emotional intelligence
Build and maintain the relationships you need to set the right tone for your project	Choosing an appropriate leadership style

Continued on next page

Enhancing Your Emotional Intelligence

The only person you can completely control is yourself, but through the effective use of influencing skills you can motivate others to willingly cooperate with you. The use of power alone, even if you truly have it, may not be the best way to get things done because you may find yourself with a resistant or indifferent team.

Project managers deal with a variety of people: team members, customers, functional managers, senior management, vendors, subject matter experts, and others. Project managers who have strong interpersonal skills build better relationships with project team members and stakeholders. When you have good relationships with team members, senior management, and stakeholders, they are more likely to listen, cooperate, and be positive. When they feel that you respect them and their opinions, they are more likely to follow your lead. These behaviors are essential to the successful and efficient completion of the project.

What is the difference between influencing and negotiation (Chapter 9)? Negotiation is a method of obtaining agreement that uses communication (Chapter 8) and relationship skills that build trust and motivate the project team.

The leadership skills needed to build effective working relationships come naturally to some people, but most of us have to learn them to become successful project managers. A key set of skills is bundled in the concept of *emotional intelligence*. The characteristics of emotional intelligence include:

- Knowing your feelings and using them to make decisions that serve you

- Reading other people's emotions without their having to tell you what they are feeling

- Handling feelings in relationships with skill and harmony (for example, being able to read and communicate the overall mood of the team)

- Being able to manage your personal life without being overtaken by emotions (for example, not being paralyzed by depression or worry, or swept away by anger)

- Persisting in the face of setbacks and channeling your impulses to pursue your goals

The table on the next page is adapted from *Primal Leadership: Learning to Lead with Emotional Intelligence*, by Daniel Goleman, Richard Boyatzis, and Annie McKee (Harvard Business School Press, Boston, MA).

Components of Emotional Intelligence

Area	Competencies
Self-awareness (The ability to understand your emotions and their effect on others)	• Emotional self-awareness: the ability to read and understand your emotions • Accurate self-assessment: a realistic evaluation of your strengths and limitations • Self-confidence: a sound sense of your worth and capabilities
Self-management (The ability to control or redirect your impulses and suspend judgment; thinking before acting)	• Emotional self-control: keeping disruptive impulses and emotions under control • Transparency and trustworthiness: displaying honesty and integrity • Adaptability: skill in adjusting to change • Achievement: a drive to meet an internal standard of excellence • Initiative: readiness to seize opportunities • Optimism: seeing positive aspects
Social awareness (An awareness of others' emotions)	• Empathy: skill in sensing other people's emotions and understanding their perspectives • Organizational awareness: the ability to read the environment of organizational life, build networks, and navigate politics • Service: the ability to recognize and meet other's needs
Social skills (The ability to manage relationships with others)	• Visionary leadership: the ability to inspire others with a compelling vision • Influence: the ability to persuade others using a wide range of tactics • Developing others: the use of guidance and feedback to assist in the development of others • Communication: skill in listening and sending clear messages • Change initiation: the tendency to initiate and lead in a new direction • Conflict management: the ability to resolve conflict, obtain agreement, and create solutions • Building bonds: skill in cultivating and maintaining relationships • Teamwork and collaboration: skill in cooperation and team building

Why do it?

To improve project efficiency and results by building strong interpersonal relationships with team members.

How do I do it?

1. **Be informed about the organizational context of your project and the key players.**

   • Know where and with whom you have influence and how to gain access to decision makers. As project manager, you need to know the influential people in the organization as well as the relationships not shown on the organization chart.

2. **Understand power.**

   • Determine if the power you hold is personal or positional, and use that information to help you manage your project.

Categories of Power

Category	Source of the Power	Type of Power	Likely Response by the Team
Personal power	The leader has the skills for achieving the goal.	Expert power	Commitment
	The leader earns respect.	Referent power	Commitment
	The leader is supported by other influential members of the organization.	Network or contact power	Commitment or resistance (depending on the individuals involved)
Positional power	The leader is qualified for his or her role in the organization.	Legitimate power	Compliance
	The leader is a source of organizational rewards.	Reward power	Compliance
	The leader can withhold desired rewards.	Disciplinary power	Resistance

> *If project team members do not report directly to you, you may have only your own personal power to draw from. If so, your influence is based on your interpersonal skills and the amount of respect you have earned. If your organization is mature in its practice of project management, you may also have positional power in addition to your personal power.*

3. **Establish rapport, and build or improve personal relationships.**

- Create connections with the project stakeholders and get to know the people on your team. Say hello, smile, and highlight factors you have in common (such as family and hobbies).

- Observe others' behaviors and words and their use of language. Pay attention to and mirror the physical characteristics of the other person (e.g., their breathing, rate of speech, posture, body language, etc.) to make them feel more comfortable.

- Be sure you are aware of how any requests that you make benefit the other person, and demonstrate the benefits as tangibly as possible.

- Be honest, kind, and genuine.

- Display your empathy through effective or active listening.

- Reduce resistance. Listen to and understand any objections, and show you are willing to address them and work toward resolving them.

- Show appreciation for the efforts of others. Acknowledge people's talents and accomplishments.

Choosing an Appropriate
Leadership Style

The most effective leaders and managers use multiple leadership styles and accurately assess the most appropriate style for a given situation. By having a strong foundation in basic interpersonal skills, you will perform with greater efficiency and less stress as you facilitate project activities, solve problems, obtain informal information, and communicate with stakeholders. By adopting an appropriate leadership style, you set the tone and culture of the project for the rest of the project team.

Why do it?

To build and maintain the relationships you need to set the right tone for your project.

How do I do it?

1. Study the widely recognized leadership styles, and choose the one that is appropriate to the members of the team and the circumstances of the project (i.e., the type of project, the amount of project risk, and the skill level of the individuals on the team).

Good leaders are proficient in at least four of the six leadership styles listed on the next two pages.

Continued on next page

Leadership Styles*

Leadership Style	What the Leader Says	Use This Style:	How It Works
Coercive/ commanding (Often highly negative due to misuse)	"Do what I I tell you."	When you're dealing with problem individuals, or during a crisis or turnaround	Eases fears and gives clear direction, especially in an emergency
Authoritative/ visionary (Most strongly positive)	"Come with me."	When a new vision is needed	Moves people toward shared dreams and vision
Affiliative (Positive)	"People come first."	When you need to heal rifts or motivate people during stressful circumstances	Creates harmony and connects/ bonds people to each other
Democratic (Positive)	"What do you think?"	To get input, build buy-in, or gain consensus	Values people's input and gains commitment through participation
Pacesetting (Frequently negative if it is poorly executed; can be demoralizing if the task is impossible or unrealistic, or if team members do not have the requisite skills)	"Do as I do, now."	When you need quick results and and the team is highly motivated and competent	Sets and meets challenging and exciting goals

Continued on next page

Leadership Styles* continued

Leadership Style	What the Leader Says	Use This Style:	How It Works
Coaching (Highly positive)	"Try this."	To enhance individual development	Connects a person's wants to the organization's goals

*Adapted from *Primal Leadership: Learning to Lead with Emotional Intelligence*, by Daniel Goleman, Richard Boyatzis, and Annie McKee (Harvard Business School Press, Boston, MA).

2. **Adjust your leadership style to fit the situation.**

   • Choose the most effective style for the team, suppliers, vendors, consultants, and stakeholders.

   • You may need to adjust your style as the people on the team grow and develop.

> *Try to verify the competence of team members before you use a less-directive leadership style.*
>
> *If your project team members have multiple projects or operational job responsibilities, there may be low commitment to your project. Ask your sponsor, functional managers, or resource managers for assistance. (If the organization has authorized a project, management should support it.)*
>
> *If there are conflicting priorities, engage your sponsor in resolving the resource issue.*

Dealing With Organizational Change

Projects are temporary and unique, produce new or modified deliverables, and often include implementation and rollout. Effective project managers understand that these issues involve change, so they help stakeholders adjust to the rollout of a new or revised deliverable. *Organizational change management* is a set of skills, tools, and techniques to help those who are affected to understand and deal with change.

Why do it?

To address the effects of change on the organization, the project team, and the stakeholders, and to improve project success.

How do I do it?

1. Learn techniques to deal with the effects of organizational change.

2. Include the key ingredients of change management (i.e., an environmental assessment, a communications plan, organizational risks and responses, and deliverables and tasks that support the change after project launch) in your project management plan.

> *When asked to do something new, people often have predictable attitudes and feelings. These reactions are sometimes negative, and they affect everyone in different ways. Ways to plan for and cope with these reactions include:*

Continued on next page

Effect of Change	Technique to Cope with this Reaction
People feel awkward, ill-at-ease, and self-conscious.	Acknowledge that this reaction is normal and temporary.
People think about what they will have to give up.	Help them understand the benefits of the change.
People feel alone even if everyone else is going through the change.	Assign mentors or partners in moving through the change.
People can handle only so much change. (Some can handle more than others.)	Provide tips on how to cope with change. Remind them that things will get easier over time.
People are at different levels of readiness for change. (Some welcome it, and others are negative and cynical.)	Schedule brainstorming and problem-solving meetings to find creative ways to deal with the changes.
People believe that they don't have enough resources. (Sometimes this perception is not valid or accurate.)	Make sure that they understand that some current activities may or definitely will go away. Use data to demonstrate that there actually are enough resources.
People revert to their old behavior or methods when the pressure is off.	Continue to maintain the gain. Use metrics to demonstrate and celebrate the benefits of the new methods, systems, or deliverables.
People impose boundaries and limitations on themselves, sometimes without realizing it.	Communicate the constraints, if any, and actively remind people of the things that they can do.
People don't always ask questions. (They make assumptions and act on them without checking.)	Hold periodic "town meetings" and Q&A sessions, or publish frequently asked questions (FAQs).

Don't forget to explain "What's In It For Me?" (WIIFM), to help people accept the changes and move forward.

3. **Adopt other techniques for dealing with change.**

   • Consider implementing the change in small steps or increments.

   • Design the new product or service to be compatible with the current deliverable. Use a familiar look and feel.

   • Identify someone who is credible and familiar to team members, and have him or her explain and "sell" the new product, process, service, or system.

   • Make sure that the new product or service works right the first time and that it is reliable.

   • Offer small, simple, easy-to-try samples, trials, or previews.

   • If the new product, service, or system is not mandatory, provide a painless way to revert to the former deliverable or system if the deliverable does not work.

Holding Effective Project Team Meetings

Project teams need to meet to share project status and issues, solve problems, and make decisions. Effective meetings cover the necessary issues and are a good use of the participants' time.

Why do it?

To make team meetings productive, pleasant, effective, and efficient.

©2006 GOAL/QPC

How do I do it?

1. **Create guidelines for the timing of all project meetings, and assign specific tasks to specific people.**

    • Use a template like the one below. (Although these guidelines may seem basic, they do help you manage expectations.)

- Meetings will be held every _____ days/weeks/months.
- Meetings will be called by _____.
- Agendas will be issued at least _____ days/weeks in advance by _____.
- Meetings will be facilitated by _____.
- Evaluations of meetings will be conducted every _____ meeting.
- The scribe will issue minutes within _____ days of the meeting.

---

2. **Create guidelines for all project meetings.**

 Guidelines may also be called ground rules and may be part of a team contract. See the Project Management Memory Jogger™ *for more information on developing team ground rules.*

Sample Conduct Guidelines for Meetings

- Meetings will begin and end on time.
- Team members will come to the meetings prepared.
- Agenda items for the next meeting will be discussed at the end of each meeting.
- Off-the-subject ideas and concerns will not be discussed during the meeting, but we will keep a record of them in a separate document for later review.
- Unresolved issues will be added to an issues list.
- If a team member cannot attend a meeting, he or she will send a representative who has the authority to make decisions.
- Meeting tasks will be rotated among members.

Virtual Team Meetings

Virtual team members reside in different locations, and they usually meet via teleconferences or Web-based applications (although these do not usually allow team members to see each other).

Virtual team meetings or teleconference calls are less effective than face-to-face meetings. The participants, sitting at their desks, are likely to multi-task, diminishing their ability to pay attention. In addition, people often don't get the full meaning of a message because they can't see others' body language and facial expressions.

In spite of these drawbacks, virtual team meetings may be the only option available. To make the most of virtual meetings, follow these guidelines:

Before the meeting:

- Be specific about time zones, and include the time zones in the notice of the meeting.

- Distribute handouts, including an agenda, well in advance of the meeting. Use revision numbers and dates in file names to identify the correct version of documents.

- Distribute a brief biography or curriculum vitae (CV) of each team member and a low-resolution photo so participants can put a face with each name and voice.

- Choose variable times for meetings so that the same people aren't inconvenienced every time (if multiple time zones are involved).

- Learn and use conference call or Web-meeting management features, such as the mute feature.

Continued on next page

- Consider reserving a meeting room for the participants at each location.
- Agree on a set of ground rules, and make sure everyone has a copy.

During the meeting:

- Be on time. Have someone call missing participants to remind them that the meeting is under way.
- Test the clarity of your speech. Speak loudly and clearly into the phone.
- Open the meeting with a roll call and a review of the ground rules.
- Do not be distracted by personal business. Stick to the agenda. Use a virtual parking lot, if necessary, to record any items that are not on the agenda. (A parking lot is a piece of flipchart paper where questions or ideas are written on a sticky note and left until the topic is discussed or until the end of the meeting. Items not resolved will be added to the issues list. For more information on parking lots, see the *Project Management Memory Jogger™*.)
- Set aside any nonproject business issues, and cover them last so that those who are not involved can leave the call.
- Begin a question with the name of the person (or persons) the question is directed to.
- Be explicit about what you are referring to in handouts, using the page or paragraph number. (Paragraph numbers are helpful.)
- Do not use notes, drawings, or graphics unless all participants can see them.

Continued on next page

Don't forget to use proper phone etiquette:

• Identify yourself when speaking.

• Announce your presence on both entrance and exit.

• Put the phone on mute when you are not speaking. (This practice protects proprietary information if visitors are in the area. It also minimizes keyboard and other background noises and does not activate hold music.)

Index